Bicycle Trails

of

Illinois

3rd Edition

An American Bike Trails Publication

Bicycle Trails
of Illinois

Published by   American Bike Trails
610 Hillside Avenue
Antioch, IL 60002

Copyright 1996 by American Bike Trails
Third Edition, Revised and Updated 2002

Created by   Ray Hoven

Design by   Mary C. Rumpsa

Table of Contents

How To Use This Book.. vi

Regional County Municipal Trail Overviews

State of Illinois and Mileage between principal cities 10

North West Region 12

North East Region 14

East Central Region 16

West Central and South Regions 17

Boone and McHenry Counties 18

Crystal Lake Trails 19

Cook County..20

DuPage County 22

Lake County 24

Rockford Area..26

Trails

Algonquin Road Trail..29

Argyle Lake State Park...30

Arie Crown Bicycle Trail 31

Blackwell Forest Preserve 32

Busse Woods Bicycle Trail..33

Catlin Park 34

Centennial Trail 36

Chain O'Lakes State Park 37

Champaign County..38

Chicago Lakefront Bike Path 40

Churchill Woods Forest Preserve 42

Comlara Park..43

Constitution Trail 44

Danada Forest Preserve 45

Deer Grove Bicycle Trail 46

Delyte Morris Bicycle Way 47

Des Plaines Division..48

Des Plaines River Trail..50

Evanston Bike Paths/North Shore Channel.................................52

Fermilab Bike Trail 53

Fox River Trail 54

Fullersburg Forest Preserve 56

Fulton Bike Trail (F.A.S.T.)...57

Grand Illinois Trail 58

Grant Woods Forest Preserve 60

Great Western Trail..61

Great River Trail..62

        Ben Butterworth Pathway 62

Table of Contents

Green Bay Trail 64
Green Belt Forest Preserve..65
Greene Valley Forest Preserve 67
Heartland Pathways..68
Hennepin Canal Parkway 70
Herrick Lake Forest Preserve 72
Hononegah Recreation Path 73
I & M Canal State Trail..74
Illinois Prairie Path 77
Batavia and Geneva Spurs..77
Great Western Trail-DuPage County..................................77
Illinois Beach State Park...78
Independence Grove 79
Indian Boundry Division..80
Jane Adams Trail 82
Jubilee College State Park 83
Kankakee River State Park..84
Kickapoo State Park 85
Kishwaukee Kiwanis Pathway 86
Kiwanis Trail...87
Lincoln Prairie Trail 88
Lost Bridge Trail...89
Long Prairie Trail..90
Lowell Parkway...92
Mattoon to Charleston Trail..93
McDowell Grove 94
Forest Preserve 94
Moraine Hills State Park 95
North Branch Bicycle Trail...96
        Techny Trail 96
North Shore Path..98
Oak Brook Bike Paths...99
Old Plank Road Trail 100
Palos & Sag Valley Forest Preserve 102
        I & M Canal Trail Cook County..............................102
Palatine Trail & Bikeway...104
Peace Road Trail...105
Pecatonica Prairie Path 106
Pimiteoui Trail 107
Potawatomi Trail...108
Prairie Trail..109
Pratts Wayne Woods Forest Preserve 110
Pyramid State Park..111

Red Hills State Park 112
River Trail of Illinois..113
Robert McClory Bike Path 114
Rock Cut State Park..116
Rock River & Sportscore Recreation Path.....................117
Rock Island State Trail..118
Salt Creek Bicycle Trail..120
Stone Bridge Trail 121
Thorn Creek Forest Preserve 122
Tinley Creek Forest Preserve...123
Tunnel Hill State Trail 124
Vadalabene Bike Trail...126
Vadalabene Nature Trail 127
Vernon Hills Trails 128
Veteran Acres Park...129
Virgil L. Gilman Nature Trail 130
Waterfall Glen Forest Preserve..131
Zion Bicycle Path..132

Additional Trails

Bartlett's Trails & Bikeways...133
Belleville's Trails & Bikeways...133
Dekalb/Sycamore Trail...133
El Paso Trail..133
Heritage-Donnelley Trail 133
Humphrey Trail..134
Lake Of The Woods Trail..134
Joe Stengel Trail 134
Poplar Creek Trail 134
Pioneer Parkway...134
Newton Lake Fish & Wildlife Area....................................135
Running Deer Trail 135
Waubonsie Trail 135
Skokie Valley Trail 135
Ronald J. Foster Heritage Parkway 135

Illinois State Parks

North West Region 136
North East Region 138
East Central Region 140
West Central Region...142
South Region...144

Indices

Trail Index 146
City to Trail Index 149
County to Trail Index 155

How To Use This Book

This book provides a comprehensive, easy-to-use quick reference to most of the off-road trails throughout Illinois. It contains over 100 detailed trail maps, plus overviews covering the state sectionally, selective counties and city areas. Detail trail maps are listed alphabetically. The sectional overviews are grouped near the front, with a section cross-referencing counties and towns to trails, and a section listing many of the parks in Illinois with their pertinent information. Each trail map includes such helpful features as location and access, trail facilities, nearby communities and their populations.

Terms Used

Length Expressed in miles. Round trip mileage is normally indicated for loops.

Effort Levels *Easy* Physical exertion is not strenuous. Climbs and descents as well as technical obstacles are more minimal. Recommended for beginners.

Moderate Physical exertion is not excessive. Climbs and descents can be challenging. Expect some technical obstacles.

Difficult Physical exertion is demanding. Climbs and descents require good riding skills. Trail surface may be sandy, loose rock, soft or wet.

Directions Describes by way of directions and distances, how to get to the trail areas from roads and nearby communities.

Map Illustrative representation of a geographic area, such as a state, section, forest, park or trail complex.

Forest Typically encompasses a dense growth of trees and underbrush covering a large tract.

Park A tract of land generally including woodlands and open areas.

DNR Department of Natural Resources

Types of Biking

Mountain Fat-tired bikes are recommended. Ride may be generally flat but then wit a soft, rocky or wet surface.

Leisure Off-road gentle ride. Surface is generally paved or screened.

Tour Riding on roads with motorized traffic or on road shoulders.

Riding Tips

- Pushing in gears that are too high can push knees beyond their limits. Avoid extremes by pedaling faster rather than shifting into a higher gear.

- Keeping your elbows bent, changing your hand position frequently and wearing bicycle gloves all help to reduce the numbness or pain in the palm of the hand from long-distance riding.

- Keep you pedal rpms up on an uphill so you have reserve power if you lose speed.

- Stay in a high-gear on a level surface, placing pressure on the pedals and resting on the handle bars and saddle.

- Lower your center of gravity on a long or steep downhill run by using the quick release seat post binder and dropping the saddle height down.

- Brake intermittently on a rough surface.

- Wear proper equipment. Wear a helmet that is approved by the Snell Memorial Foundation or the American National Standards Institute. Look for one of their stickers inside the helmet.

- Use a lower tire inflation pressure for riding on unpaved surfaces. The lower pressure will provide better tire traction and a more comfortable ride.

- Apply your brakes gradually to maintain control on loose gravel or soil.

- Ride only on trails designated for bicycles or in areas where you have the permission of the landowner.

- Be courteous to hikers or horseback riders on the trail, they have the right of way.

- Leave riding trails in the condition you found them. Be sensitive to the environment. Properly dispose of your trash. If you open a gate, close it behind you.

- Don't carry items or attach anything to your bicycle that might hinder your vision or control.

- Don't wear anything that restricts your hearing.

- Don't carry extra clothing where it can hang down and jam in a wheel.

Explanation of Symbols

ROUTES

——— Biking Trail

▬▬▬ Bikeway

▬ ▬ ▬ Alternate Bike Trail

■ ■ ■ Alternate Use Trail

= = = Planned Trail

——— Roadway

FACILITIES

🔧 Bike Repair

🅰 Camping

➕ First Aid

❓ Info

🛏 Lodging

🅿 Parking

🏕 Picnic

🍴 Refreshments

🚻 Restrooms

🏠 Shelter

🚰 Water

MF Multi Facilities
Available

Refreshments   First Aid
Telephone   Picnic
Restrooms   Lodging

TRAIL USES

🚵 Mountain Biking

🚲 Leisure Biking

⛸ In Line Skating

⛷ (X-C) Cross-Country
Skiing

🚶 Hiking

🐴 Horseback Riding

🛷 Snowmobiling

ROAD RELATED SYMBOLS

(45) Interstate Highway

(45) U.S. Highway

(45) State Highway

45 County Highway

AREA DESCRIPTIONS

■ Parks, Schools,
Preserves, etc.

■ Waterway

▬ Mileage Scale

✦ Directional

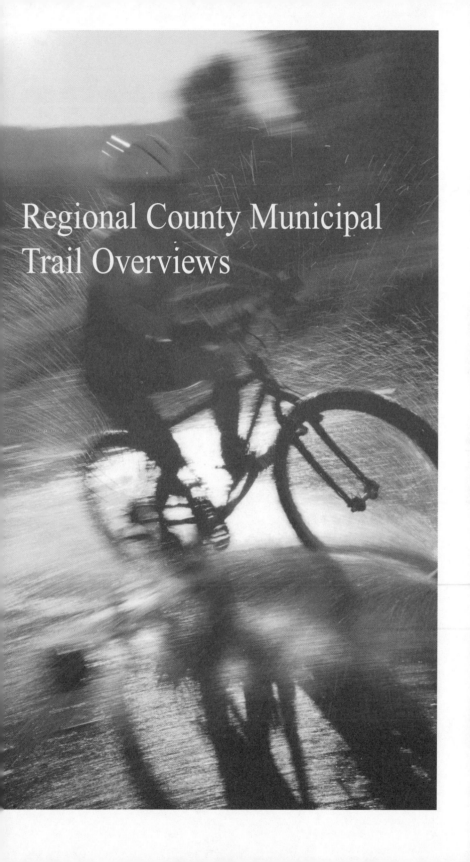

Regional County Municipal Trail Overviews

State of Illinois

American Bike Trails

Mileage between principal cities

CITY	SPRINGFIELD	ST. LOUIS, MO	ROCKFORD	PEORIA	CHICAGO	CHAMPAIGN
BLOOMINGTON	64	163	136	40	136	53
CAIRO	242	148	426	312	375	244
CARBONDALE	172	108	384	242	333	202
CHAMPAIGN	86	182	188	92	137	
CHICAGO	201	300	83	170		137
DECATUR	39	118	179	83	178	47
DE KALB	183	282	44	124	66	174
DUBUQUE, IA	238	337	91	167	176	259
EFFINGHAM	89	104	260	164	209	78
ELGIN	208	307	48	148	37	169
GALESBURG	120	219	150	49	198	141
KANKAKEE	158	254	138	121	56	78
LAWRENCEVILLE	154	147	309	213	250	127
MOLINE	163	262	117	92	165	184
MT. VERNON	146	82	330	216	279	148
PEORIA	71	170	138		170	92
QUINCY	110	133	269	131	310	195
ROCKFORD	197	296		138	83	188
ST. LOUIS, MO	100		296	170	300	182
SPRINGFIELD		100	197	71	201	86
WAUKEGAN	229	328	71	198	40	181

State of Illinois

North West Region

No.	**Trail Name**	**Page #**
1.)	Rock Cut State Park	116
2.)	Hononegah Recreation Path	73
3.)	Stone Bridge Trail	121
4.)	Rock River & Sportscore Recreation Path	117
5.)	Pecatonica Prairie Path	106
6.)	Lowell Parkway	92
7.)	Fulton Bike Trail (F.A.S.T.)	57
8.)	Great River Trail	62
9.)	Ben Butterworth Pathway	62
10.)	Kiwanis Trail	87
11.)	Hennepin Canal Parkway	70
12.)	Jane Adams Trails	82
13.)	Rock Island State Trail	118
14.)	Pimiteoui Trail	107
15.)	River Trail of Illinois	113
16.)	Pioneer Parkway	134
17.)	Perryville & Willow Creek Paths	26
18.)	Jubilee College State Park	83
19.)	Potawatomi Trail	108
20.)	Joe Stengel Trail	134
21.)	Running Deer Trail	135

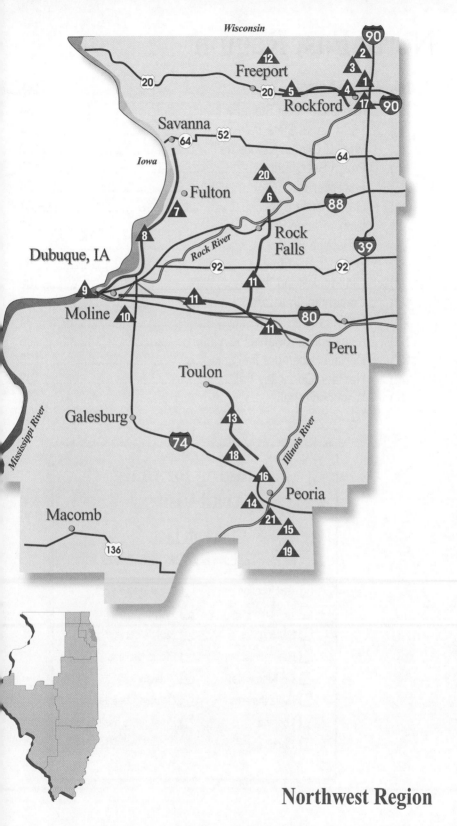

Wisconsin

12

Freeport

20

20

90

2

3

1

4

5

17

90

Rockford

Savanna

52

64

64

Iowa

20

Fulton

6

7

88

Rock
Falls

8

Rock River

39

Dubuque, IA

92

92

9

11

Moline

11

10

80

11

Peru

Toulon

Galesburg

74

13

Illinois River

18

16

Peoria

14

Macomb

21

15

136

19

Northwest Region

North East Region

No.	Trail Name	Page #
1.)	Kankakee River State Park	84
2.)	I & M Canal State Trail	74
3.)	Virgil L. Gilman Nature Trail	130
4.)	Peace Road Trail	105
5.)	Fox River Trail	54
6.)	Great Western Trail	61
7.)	Illinois Prairie Path	76
	Batavia Spur	76
8.)	Fermilab Bike Trail	53
9.)	Old Plank Road Trail	100
10.)	Centennial Trail	36
11.)	Catlin Park	34
12.)	Kishwaukee Kiwanis Pkwy	86
13.)	DeKalb/Sycamore Trail	133
14.)	Heritage Donnelley Trail	133
15.)	Waubonsie Trail	135

Planning for that Trail Visit

Checkoff List

Information you may want to have at hand

- ☐ Trail location
- ☐ Trail accesses
- ☐ Parking
- ☐ Restrooms
- ☐ Drinking water
- ☐ Refreshments
- ☐ Lodging
- ☐ Conditions
- ☐ Local area events
- ☐ Telephone access
- ☐ Bicycle service
- ☐ Picnic facilities
- ☐ Shelters
- ☐ Camping facilities
- ☐ Emergency assistance phone number

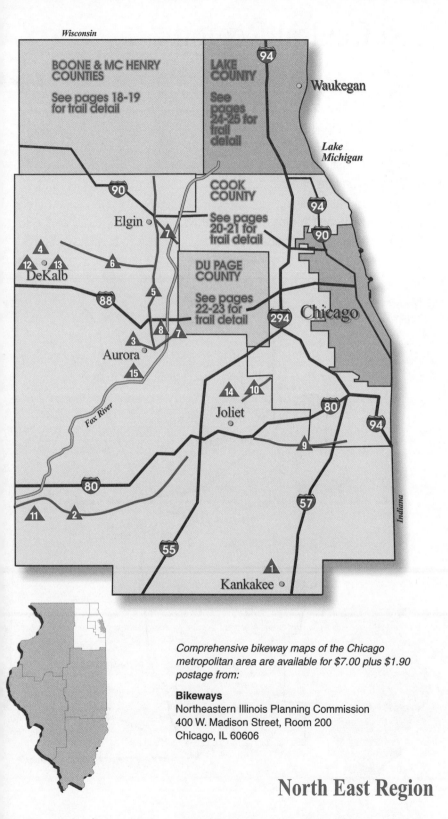

Wisconsin

BOONE & MC HENRY COUNTIES

See pages 18-19 for trail detail

LAKE COUNTY

See pages 24-25 for trail detail

Waukegan

Lake Michigan

COOK COUNTY

See pages 20-21 for trail detail

Elgin

DU PAGE COUNTY

See pages 22-23 for trail detail

DeKalb

Chicago

Aurora

Fox River

Joliet

Kankakee

Indiana

Comprehensive bikeway maps of the Chicago metropolitan area are available for $7.00 plus $1.90 postage from:

Bikeways
Northeastern Illinois Planning Commission
400 W. Madison Street, Room 200
Chicago, IL 60606

North East Region

East Central Region

No.	Trail Name	Page #
1.)	Kickapoo State Park	85
2.)	Champaign County	38
3.)	Heartland Pathways	68
4.)	Constitution Trail	44
5.)	Comlara Park	43
6.)	El Paso Trail	133
7.)	Mattoon/Charleston Bike Path	93
8.)	Lake of the Woods	134

West Central and South Regions

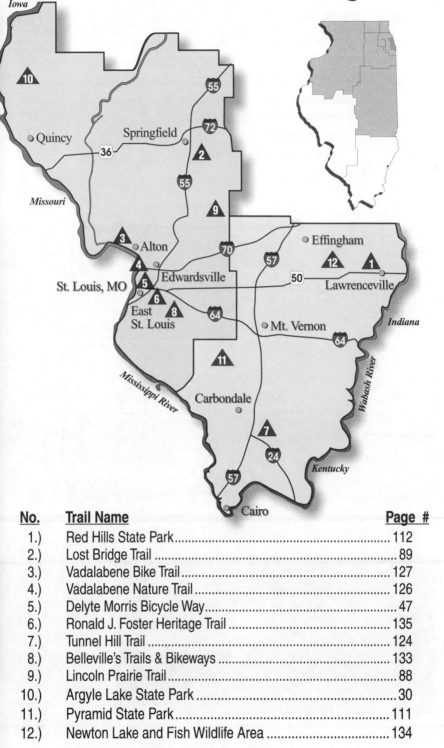

No.	Trail Name	Page #
1.)	Red Hills State Park	112
2.)	Lost Bridge Trail	89
3.)	Vadalabene Bike Trail	127
4.)	Vadalabene Nature Trail	126
5.)	Delyte Morris Bicycle Way	47
6.)	Ronald J. Foster Heritage Trail	135
7.)	Tunnel Hill Trail	124
8.)	Belleville's Trails & Bikeways	133
9.)	Lincoln Prairie Trail	88
10.)	Argyle Lake State Park	30
11.)	Pyramid State Park	111
12.)	Newton Lake and Fish Wildlife Area	134

Boone and McHenry Counties

No.	Trail Name	Page #
1.)	Long Prairie Trail	90
2.)	Prairie Trail	109
3.)	Moraine Hills State Park	95
4.)	Crystal Lake Trails	19
	Veteran Acres Park	129
	Walt Herrick Trail	19
	Winding Creek Bike Trail	19
5.)	Fox River Trail	54

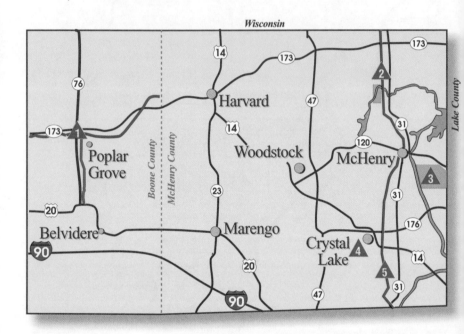

Crystal Lake Trails

	•Prairie Trail	•Sterne's Woods	•Veteran Acres	W. Herrick Lippold Pk.	Winding Creek
Trail Length	18 mi.	2.1 mi.	7.5 mi.	3.5 mi.	2.5 mi.
Surface	pvd./scrn'g	paved/dirt road	paved/natural	screenings	paved
Uses*	L, H	F, H, X	F, H, X	L, H	L, S

Location & Setting — These trails are located throughout the Crystal Lake area. McHenry County is a favorite destination for water sport activities by Chicagoland residents.

Information — Crystal Lake Park District (815) 459-0680
One East Crystal Lake Avenue
Crystal Lake, IL 60014

County — McHenry

•*See Detail Maps*

* USES	F = Fat Tire Bicycling	H = Hiking, Jogging L
L = Leisure Bicycling	S = in-line skating	X = Cross country skiing

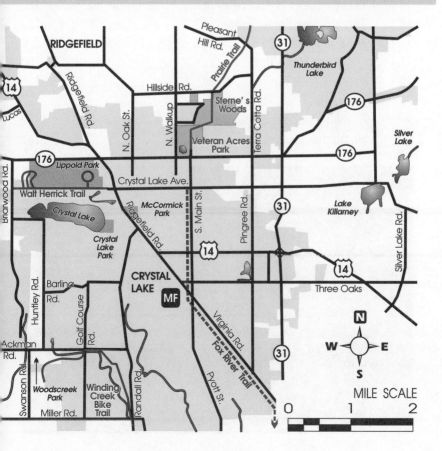

19

Cook County

No.	Trail Name	Page #
1.)	Deer Grove Bicycle Trail	46
2.)	Palatine Trail & Bikeway	104
3.)	Busse Woods Bicycle Trail	33
4.)	Des Plaines Division	48
5.)	Techny Trail	97
6.)	North Branch Bicycle Trail	96
7.)	Green Bay Trail	64
8.)	Evanston Bike Paths/North Shore Channel	52
9.)	Chicago Lakefront Bike Path	40
10.)	Indian Boundry Division	80
11.)	Salt Creek Bicycle Trail	120
12.)	Arie Crown Bicycle Trail	31
13.)	I & M Canal Trail—Cook County	103
14.)	Palos & Sag Valley Forest Preserve	102
15.)	Tinley Creek Forest Preserve	123
16.)	Thorn Creek Forest Preserve	122
17.)	Illinois Prairie Path	76
18.)	Old Plank Road Trail	100
19.)	Poplar Creek Trail	135
20.)	Algonquin Road Trail	29
21.)	Bartlett's Trails and Bikeways	133
22.)	Humphrey Trail	134

American Bike Trails

Palatine

1
2
20

94
41
294
94
14
5
6
7
4
294
8
Evanston
3
355
Elk Grove
Village
9
Lake
Michigan
10
90
290
11
94
Elmhurst
17
88
55
290
DuPage County
294
55
12
Chicago
13
14
Oak
Lawn
22
294
90
94
Tinley
Park
15
16
80
Chicago
Heights
18
394
Indiana
19
90
20
21

Cook County

DuPage County

No.	Trail Name	Page #
1.)	Pratts Wayne Woods Forest Preserve	110
2.)	Illinois Prairie Path	76
3.)	Blackwell Forest Preserve	32
4.)	Herrick Lake Forest Preserve	72
5.)	McDowell Grove Forest Preserve	94
6.)	Greene Valley Forest Preserve	67
7.)	Danada Forest Preserve	45
8.)	Churchill Woods Forest Preserve	42
9.)	Great Western Trail - DuPage County	76
10.)	Fullersburg Forest Preserve	56
11.)	Oak Brook Bike Paths	99
12.)	Waterfall Glen Forest Preserve	131

Bicycle Resources

Bicycling *(Brochure)* Free

Illinois Department of Conservation
Office of Resource Marketing and Education
524 South Second Street
Springfield, IL 62701-1787

(217)782-7454

Information brochure listing off-road bicycle trails statewide. The Department of Conservation also distributes an attractive Illinois State Parks magazine as well as brochures on hiking, camping, and other outdoor activities.

Illinois Visitor's Guide

Illinois Dept. of Commerce and Community Affairs
Bureau of Tourism
620 East Adams Street
Springfield, IL 62701

(800)223-0121

Lists campgrounds, hotels and motels, and recreational and cultural attractions throughout the state.

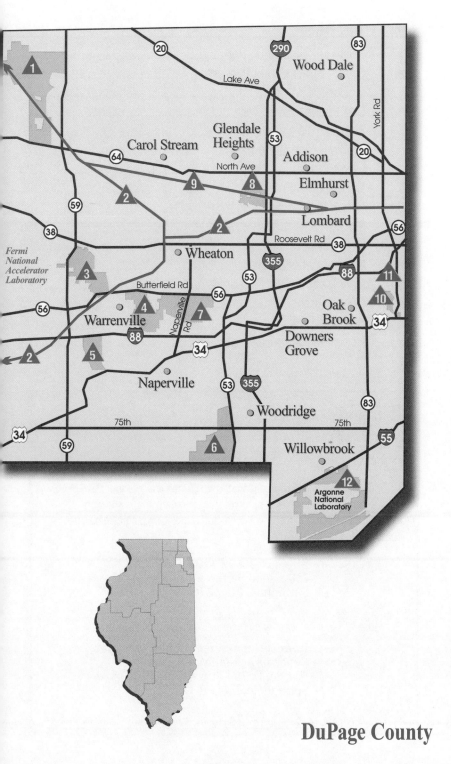

DuPage County

Lake County

No.	Trail Name	Page #
1.)	Chain O'Lakes State Park	37
2.)	Grant Woods Forest Preserve	60
3.)	McDonald Woods	25
4.)	Des Plaines River Trail	50
5.)	Zion Bicycle Path	132
6.)	Illinois Beach State Park	78
7.)	Lyons Woods	25
8.)	North Shore Path	98
9.)	Green Belt Forest Preserve	65
10.)	Skokie Valley Trail	135
11.)	Vernon Hills Trails	128
12.)	Independence Grove	50
13.)	Lincolnshire Civic Center Path	25
14.)	Cuba Marsh	25
15.)	Buffalo Creek	25
16.)	Robert McClory Bike Path	114

Bicycle Resources

BIKE TOURING INFORMATION

The State of Illinois recommends that when planning a bike tour the Department of Transportation be contacted for county maps showing low-volume local roads along your selected route. A map catalog can be obtained from:

Map Sales
Illinois Dept. of Transportation
2300 South Dirksen Parkway
Springfield, IL 62764

For more information concerning other trail activities, please contact:

Illinois Department of Conservation
Office of Public Information
524 South 2nd Street
Springfield, IL 62701-1787

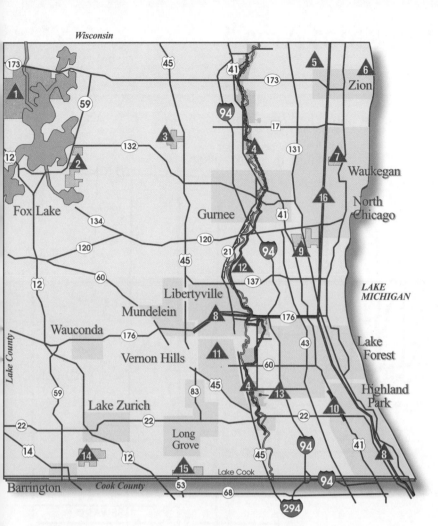

Bicycle Maintenance Checklist
Inspect your bicycle for the following:

Tires should not have cracks on the sidewalls, cuts in the tread or excessive wear. Using proper tire pressure, printed on the sidewall of the tire, prevents excessive wear.

Gear and brake cables move freely. Replace rusted or frayed cables.

The chain should be free of rust. Too much oil will attract dust and dirt, shortening the life of the chain.

Pedals are securely fastened, and pedal reflectors are clean and visible.

This checklist takes only a few minutes and may prevent you from having an accident or mechanical breakdown.

Lake County

Rockford Area

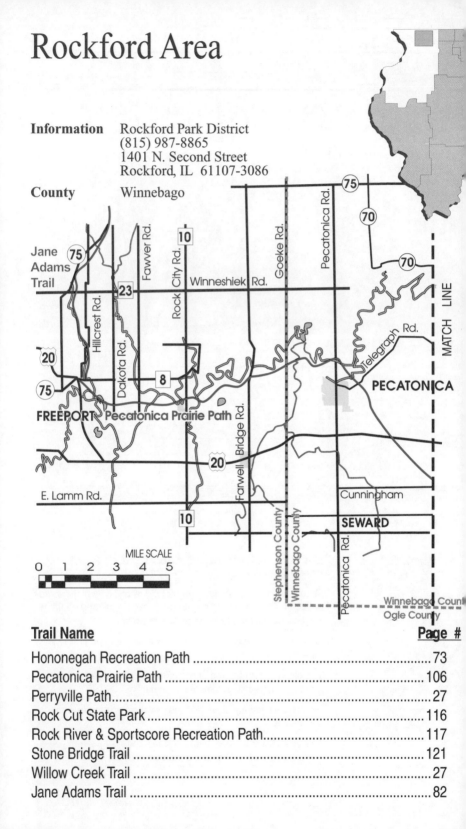

Information   Rockford Park District
(815) 987-8865
1401 N. Second Street
Rockford, IL 61107-3086

County   Winnebago

Trail Name	Page #
Hononegah Recreation Path	73
Pecatonica Prairie Path	106
Perryville Path	27
Rock Cut State Park	116
Rock River & Sportscore Recreation Path	117
Stone Bridge Trail	121
Willow Creek Trail	27
Jane Adams Trail	82

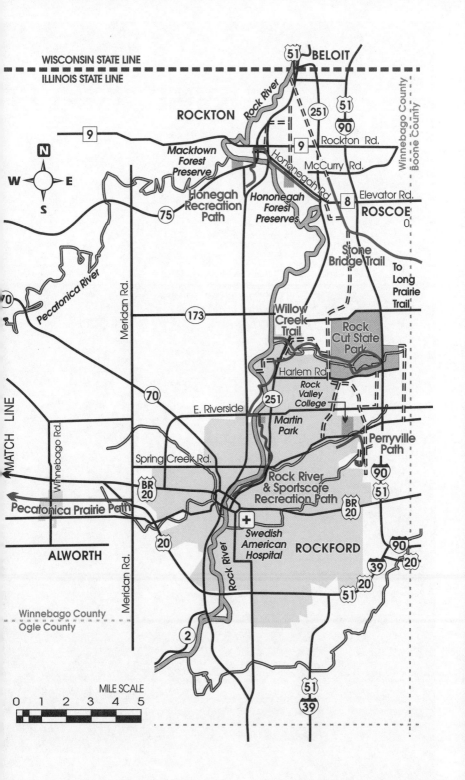

Rockford Area

Trails

Algonquin Road Trail

Trail Length	9.5 miles
Surface	Paved
Uses	Leisure bicycling, hiking/jogging
Location & Setting	The Algonquin Trail is located in northwest Cook County. It runs from Harper College west to Potawami Woods at Stover and Palatine Roads. The trail generally parallels Algonquin Road, but there is a 6 mile loop around the parameter of the Paul Douglas Forest Preserve and the Highland Woods Golf Course south of Algonquin Road. The setting is open and urban, and wooded as you enter the Forest Preserve.
Information	Cook County Forest Preserve (708) 366-9420
County	Cook

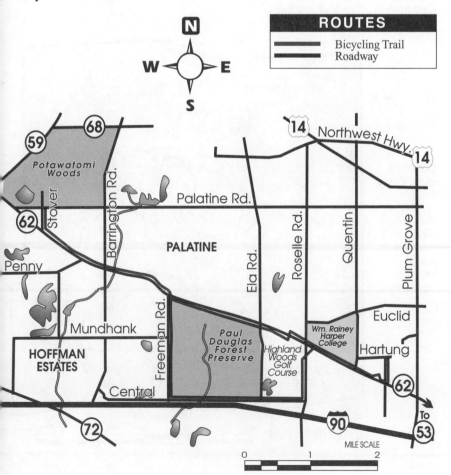

Argyle Lake State Park

Trail Length	7 miles
Surface	Natural – groomed
Uses	Fat tire bicycling, cross-country skiing, hiking, horseback riding, snowmobiling
Location & Setting	From Macomb, west on Rte 136 to Colchester, then north on 500E to the park entrance. Argyle Lake State Park is located about 7-miles west of Macomb, and offers picnicking, camping, and boating in addition to a scenic and rugged 7-mile trail for mountain biking and horseback riding. Effort level is moderate to difficult. There is a concession stand near the boat dock. Class, A, B, C and D campsites are available.
Information	Argyle Lake State Park (309) 776-3422
County	McDonough

The Park's Visitor Center features wildlife displays and educational materials along with park information.

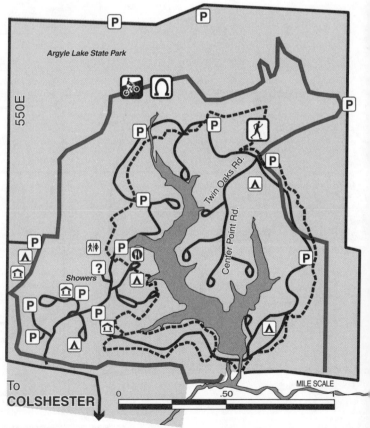

Arie Crown Bicycle Trail

Trail Length	3.2 miles
Surface	Packed dirt
Uses	Fat tire bicycling, cross country skiing, hiking
Location & Setting	Located in south Cook County near Countryside and north of the Palos Forest Preserve. Access at Brainard and Joliet Roads or LaGrange Road, north of 67th Street. Woods, open areas.
Information	Forest Preserve District of Cook County (708) 366-8420
County	Cook

EMERGENCY ASSISTANCE
Forest Preserve Police .... (708) 366-8210
or .... (708) 366-8211

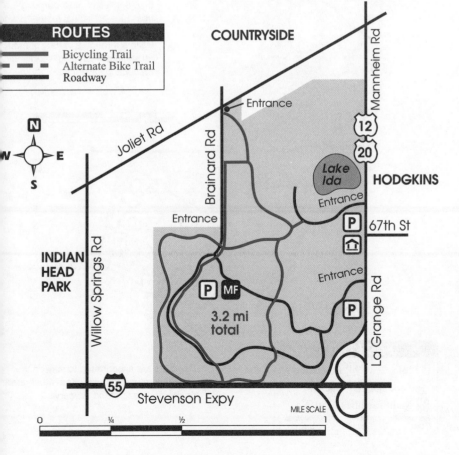

ROUTES
- Bicycling Trail
- Alternate Bike Trail
- Roadway

COUNTRYSIDE

Mannheim Rd

Joliet Rd

Brainard Rd

Entrance

12
20

Lake Ida

HODGKINS

Entrance

N
W E
S

Entrance

P 67th St

Willow Springs Rd

INDIAN HEAD PARK

Entrance

P MF

3.2 mi total

La Grange Rd

P

55 Stevenson Expy

MILE SCALE

0   ¼   ½   1

Blackwell Forest Preserve

Trail Length	3.3 miles leisure, 8.3 miles total
Surface	Limestone screenings, natural groomed
Uses	Leisure and fat tire bicycling.cross country skiing, hiking/jogging (horseback riding is restricted)
Location & Setting	The Blackwell Preserve, located between Winfield and Warrenville in west central DuPage County, can be accessed from Butterfield Road, 1 mile west of Route 59 or from Mack Road, ¼ miles east of Route 59.
Information	Forest Preserve District of DuPage County (630) 790-4900
County	DuPage

The Blackwell Preserve has more than 8 miles of multi-purpose trails plus additional footpaths and unmarked trails. The trails lead visitors through a variety of natural settings, including woodlands, marsh and savannas.

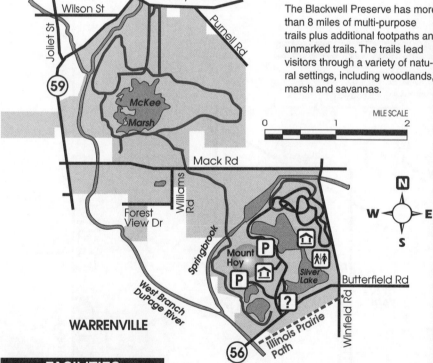

Bicyclists are encouraged to stay on the designated trails in the McKee Marsh area on the north end of the Preserve.

Busse Woods Bicycle Trail

Trail Length	11.2 miles
Surface	Paved
Uses	Leisure bicycling, in-line skating, cross country skiing, hiking/jogging
Location & Setting	Located in northwest Cook County in the Ned Brown Preserve, bordered on the north by Arlington Heights and to the east by Elk Grove Village. Wooded areas, open spaces and small lakes.
Information	Forest Preserve District of Cook County (708) 366-9420
County	Cook

The Ned Brown Preserve is a 3700 acre holding, and surrounds Busse Lake, a 590 acre lake that serves as the focal point of the area.

The bicycle trail winds through the forests and meadows around Busse Lake providing access to many of the preserves unique features.

Trail accesses include Golf Road at Hwy. 90, Arlington Heights Road and Higgins, and at Biesterfield Road and Bisner Road.

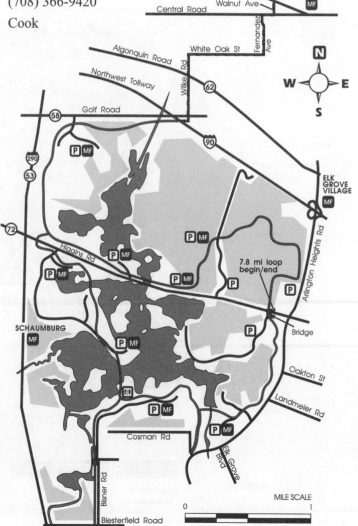

33

Catlin Park

Trail Length	13 miles
Surface	Natural – groomed
Uses	Fat tire bicycling, hiking, horseback riding, cross-country skiing
Location & Setting	Catlin Park is an earth and grass system of criss-crossing loop trails located SW of Ottawa and just E of Starved Rock State Park. Effort level is moderate. Facilities include restrooms, picnic areas and fishing ponds.

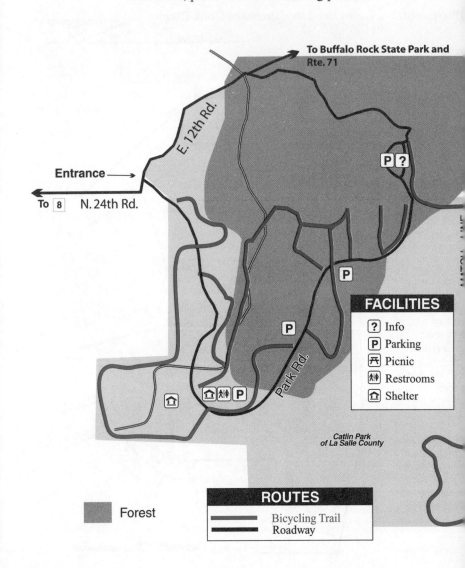

To Buffalo Rock State Park and Rte. 71

E. 12th Rd.

Entrance →

To 8 N. 24th Rd.

Park Rd.

Catlin Park
of La Salle County

FACILITIES

? Info
P Parking
🎪 Picnic
🚻 Restrooms
🏠 Shelter

Forest

ROUTES

Bicycling Trail
Roadway

Information   LaSalle County Parks Dept
RR# 2560 E 1251 SR
Ottawa, IL 61350

County   LaSalle

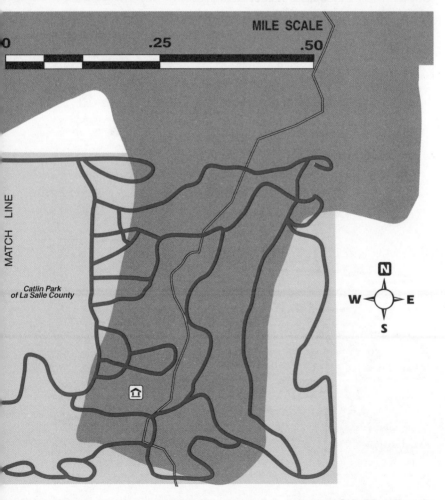

MILE SCALE

0   .25   .50

MATCH LINE

*Catlin Park
of La Salle County*

N
W E
S

Catlin Park

Centennial Trail

Trail Length	20 miles
Surface	Crushed Stone
Uses	Leisure bicycling, hiking, cross-country skiing
Location & Setting	This 20-mile trail runs from the Chicago Portage site at Lyons in Cook County to Lockport in Will County, and forms a link in the Grand Illinois Trail. The surface is crushed limestone and is 10-feet wide. Setting is suburban with most services readily accessible.
Information	Cook County Forest Preserve (708) 336-9420
County	Cook, DuPage, Will

FACILITIES

MF Multi Facilities Available

Refreshments   First Aid
Telephone   Picnic
Restrooms   Lodging

Chain O'Lakes State Park

Trail Length	5.0 miles
Surface	Limestone screenings
Uses	Leisure bicycling, cross country skiing, hiking, horseback riding
Location & Setting	Chain O'Lakes State Park is a 2,793 acre park located at the northwest corner of Lake County. Woods, open park areas.
Information	Chain O'Lakes State Park (847) 587-5512
County	Lake

In addition to bicycling, other activities include boating, fishing, picnicking, and camping. Horses and boats can be rented.

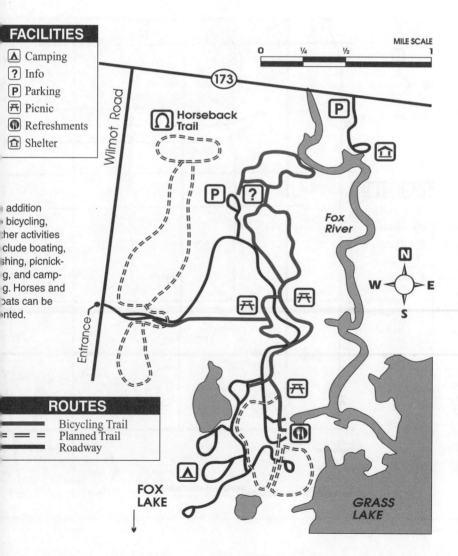

FACILITIES

- Ⓐ Camping
- ? Info
- Ⓟ Parking
- 🐾 Picnic
- Ⓜ Refreshments
- 🏠 Shelter

ROUTES

- ——— Bicycling Trail
- = = = Planned Trail
- ━━━ Roadway

Champaign County

Trail Length	Approximately 18 miles of bike path (plus over 30 miles of bike routes)
Surface	Paved
Uses	Leisure bicycling, in-line skating, hiking/jogging

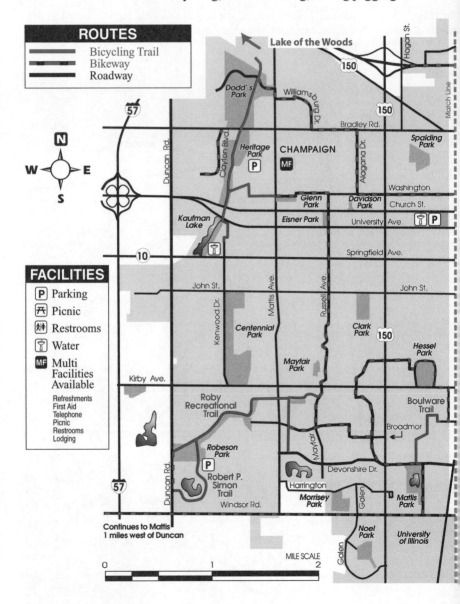

ROUTES
- Bicycling Trail
- Bikeway
- Roadway

FACILITIES
- P Parking
- 🛆 Picnic
- 🚻 Restrooms
- 🜄 Water
- MF Multi Facilities Available
  - Refreshments
  - First Aid
  - Telephone
  - Picnic
  - Restrooms
  - Lodging

Lake of the Woods

CHAMPAIGN

Dodd's Park
Williamsburg Dr.
Bradley Rd.
Spalding Park
Heritage Park
Washington
Glenn Park
Davidson Park
Church St.
Kaufman Lake
Eisner Park
University Ave.
Springfield Ave.
John St.
John St.
Centennial Park
Clark Park
Hessel Park
Mayfair Park
Kirby Ave.
Roby Recreational Trail
Boulware Trail
Broadmor
Robeson Park
Robert P. Simon Trail
Devonshire Dr.
Harrington
Matlis Park
Morrisey Park
Windsor Rd.
Noel Park
University of Illinois

Duncan Rd.
Clayton Blvd.
Alabama Dr.
Hagan St.
Mattis Ave.
Russell Ave.
Kenwood Dr.
Mayfair
Galen
Galen
Match Line

Continues to Mattis
1 miles west of Duncan

MILE SCALE
0   1   2

Location & Setting	The cities of Champaign and Urbana in east central Illinois. The paths generally parallel streets or through parks. The setting is urban and is the home of the University of Illinois.
Information	Champaign County Regional Planning Commission (217) 328-3313
County	Champaign

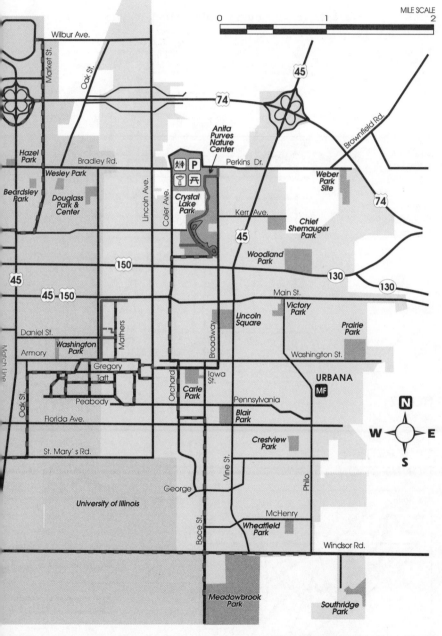

Champaign County

Chicago Lakefront Bike Path

Trail Length	Approximately 20 miles	
Surface	Paved	
Uses	Leisure bicycling, in-line skating, jogging	

Northern Section

Parking, accesses, restrooms, water, and refreshments located throughout the bikeway.

N
W — E
S

NORTH BRANCH TO LAKEFRONT BIKE PATH CONNECTION

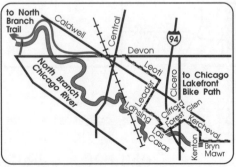

MATCH LIN

MILE SCA

0   1   2

FACILITIES

🔧 Bike Repair

Location & Setting	From the north, the bike path begins around Bryn Mawr (5600 north) and Sheridan Road, then proceeds south along the shoreline of Lake Michigan to 71st Street. Urban lakefront.
Information	Chicago Park District
County	Cook

(312) 747-2200

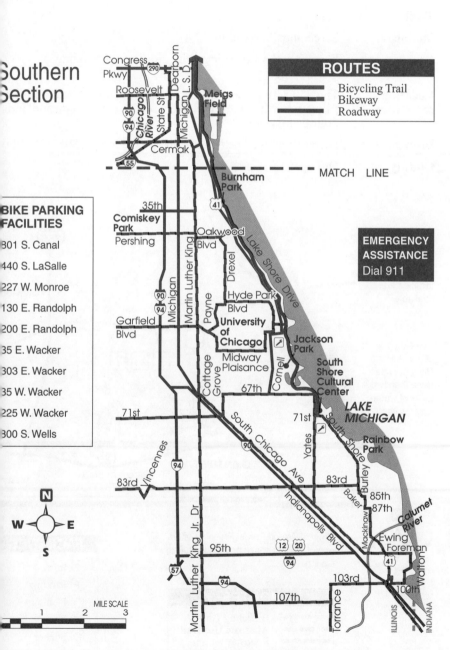

Southern Section

ROUTES
- Bicycling Trail
- Bikeway
- Roadway

EMERGENCY ASSISTANCE
Dial 911

BIKE PARKING FACILITIES
- 301 S. Canal
- 440 S. LaSalle
- 227 W. Monroe
- 130 E. Randolph
- 200 E. Randolph
- 35 E. Wacker
- 303 E. Wacker
- 35 W. Wacker
- 225 W. Wacker
- 300 S. Wells

MILE SCALE

Chicago Lakefront Bike Path

41

Churchill Woods Forest Preserve

Trail Length	3.8 miles
Surface	Screenings, mowed turf
Uses	Leisure and fat tire bicycling, cross country skiing, hiking/jogging
Location & Setting	The 259 acre preserve is located between Lombard and Glen Ellyn in north central DuPage County. Setting is woodlands, prairie and river.
Information	Forest Preserve District of DuPage County (630) 790-4900
County	DuPage

Picnicking is popular and camping facilities are available.

The east branch of the DuPage River provides more than two miles of waterway frontage.

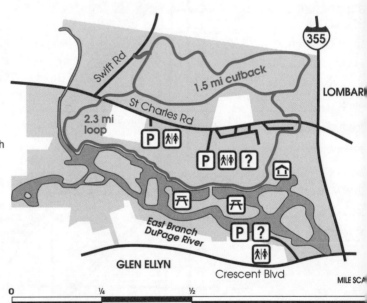

Churchill Wood Forest Preserve offers one of the last native prairies in DuPage County.

ROUTES

——	Bicycling Trail
– – –	Alternate Use Trail
——	Roadway

FACILITIES

?	Info
P	Parking
🔺	Picnic
🚻	Restrooms
🏠	Shelter

Comlara Park

Trail Length	10.5 miles
Surface	Natural turf
Uses	Fat tire bicycling (easy to difficult), hiking
Location & Setting	Located in north central Illinois approximately 12 miles north of Bloomington/Normal. The several trails encompass Evergreen Lake. Setting is wooded with lakefront and hills.
Information	McLean County Parks and Recreation (309) 726-2022
County	McLean

No water or restrooms are available on these trails.

Trails are restricted to single file, are natural turf surface, and are continually changing and variable.

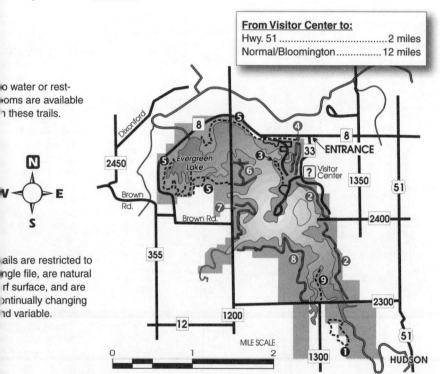

From Visitor Center to:
Hwy. 51 ....2 miles
Normal/Bloomington................12 miles

MILE SCALE

No.	Trail Name	Miles	Effort Level
1.	Shady Hollow Nature Trail *	1.00	Easy
2.	Deer Island Area Access Trail	2.50	Difficult
3.	Hickory Grove Nature Trail *	.50	Easy
4.	Campers Park Access Trail	1.50	Moderate
5.	Lakeview Area Access Trail	3.00	Moderate
6.	White Oak Area Access Trail	.50	Easy
7.	Two Cedars Prairie Access Trail	.50	Easy
8.	Southern Zone Access Trail	2.50	Moderate
9.	Mallard Cove Access Trail *	.25	Moderate

Foot traffic only

Constitution Trail

Trail Length	10 miles
Surface	Paved asphalt
Uses	Leisure bicycling, in-line skating, cross country skiing, jogging
Location & Setting	Located in Bloomington & Normal. The setting is parkways through urban areas.
Information	McLean County Chamber of Commerce (309) 829-1641
	McLean County Wheelers Bicycle Club (309) 454-1541
	Friends of the Constitution Trail P.O. Box 4494 L Bloomington, IL 61702
	Bloomington Parks & Recreation Dept. (309) 454-9540
County	McClean

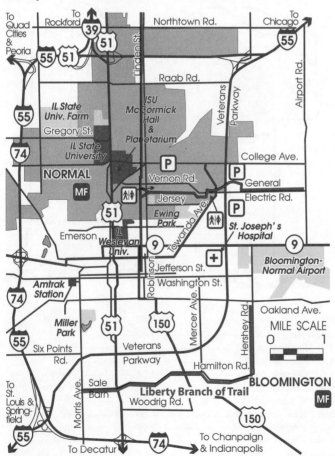

The trail is built on abandoned trail bed and runs through business and residential areas. The north south segment is wooded with patches of prairie on the eastern section. Trail accesses from numerous street connections.

Picnic tables and benches are located along the trail. Both Illinois State University and Wesleyan University are located within a short distance of the trail.

Open from dawn to dusk.

Danada Forest Preserve

Trail Length	2.0 miles of bicycling trails, 2.9 miles total
Surface	Limestone screenings
Uses	Leisure bicycling, cross country skiing, hiking jogging, horseback riding
Location & Setting	Danada Forest Preserve located in the city of Wheaton in central DuPage County, can be accessed from Naperville Road, ½ mile north of Interstate 88. Prairie, woodland, and marsh.
Information	Forest Preserve District of DuPage County (630) 790-4900 Danada Forest Preserves (630) 933-7248
County	DuPage

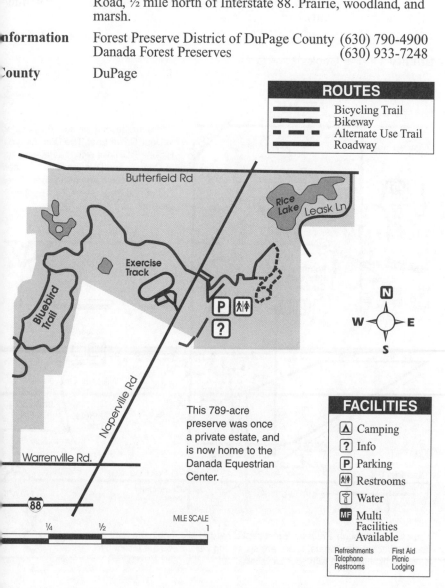

ROUTES
- Bicycling Trail
- Bikeway
- Alternate Use Trail
- Roadway

This 789-acre preserve was once a private estate, and is now home to the Danada Equestrian Center.

FACILITIES
- ▲ Camping
- ? Info
- P Parking
- 🕴🕴 Restrooms
- 🍸 Water
- **MF** Multi Facilities Available

Refreshments   First Aid
Telephone   Picnic
Restrooms   Lodging

MILE SCALE

Deer Grove Bicycle Trail

Trail Length	4.0 miles
Surface	Paved
Uses	Leisure bicycling, x-c skiing, jogging/hiking
Location & Setting	The Deer Grove Preserve consists of rolling upland forest interspersed with wooded ravines and wetlands. Creeks meander through the tract, feeding two lakes located in the preserve. Open spaces, wooded areas (connects to Palatine Trail).
Information	Forest Preserve District of Cook County (708) 366-9420
County	Cook

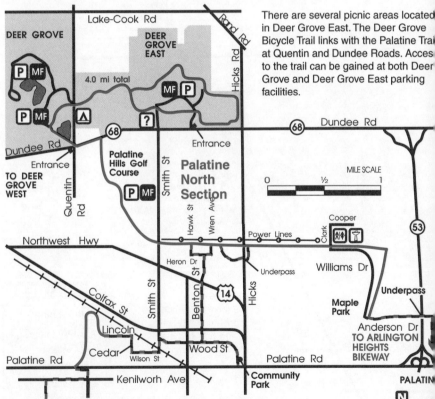

There are several picnic areas located in Deer Grove East. The Deer Grove Bicycle Trail links with the Palatine Trail at Quentin and Dundee Roads. Access to the trail can be gained at both Deer Grove and Deer Grove East parking facilities.

You can ride through a mature forest past a herd of elk, then head for the lake to watch the sailboats. There are six fishing walls if you are inclined to do some fishing along with your bicycling.

Delyte Morris Bicycle Way

Trail Length	5 miles (2.6 path and 2.4 streets)
Surface	Paved and crushed stone
Uses	Leisure bicycling, hiking
Location & Setting	This bicycle way goes from the courthouse in Edwardsville to Bluff Road on the western edge of the Southern Illinois University campus. From Edwardsville the trail proceeds down a small valley and through some heavily wooded area. Sections are rugged with hilly terrain. Once out of the woods, it follows an old railroad right-of-way, through prairie areas and the grade is easy.
Information	Campus Recreation Southern Illinois University (618) 692-3235
County	Madison

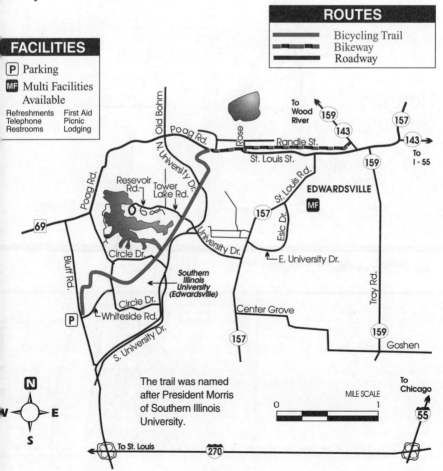

FACILITIES

P Parking

MF Multi Facilities
Available

Refreshments	First Aid
Telephone	Picnic
Restrooms	Lodging

ROUTES

Bicycling Trail
Bikeway
Roadway

The trail was named after President Morris of Southern Illinois University.

MILE SCALE

0   1

47

Des Plaines Division

Trail Length	12 miles
Surface	Natural groomed (5 to 10 feet wide)
Uses	Fat tire bicycling, hiking, horseback riding
Location & Setting	Located along the east bank of the Des Plaines River in northwest Cook County. It begins at Touhy Avenue, east of Mannheim Road, and continues north to the Lake-Cook County line. The setting is river bottom with woods, open areas and small hills.
Information	Emergency Assistance - Call 911 Cook County Forest Preserve District (708) 366-8420
County	Cook

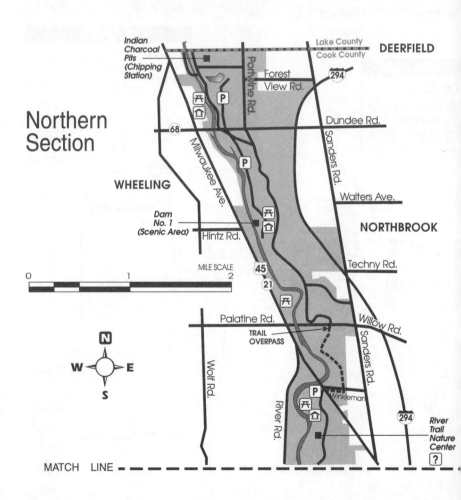

Northern Section

Indian Charcoal Pits (Chipping Station)

Lake County
Cook County
DEERFIELD
Forest View Rd.
294
Dundee Rd.
Portwine Rd.
68
Milwaukee Ave.
WHEELING
Sanders Rd.
Walters Ave.
Dam No. 1 (Scenic Area)
Hintz Rd.
NORTHBROOK
Techny Rd.
MILE SCALE
0   1   2
45
21
Palatine Rd.
Willow Rd.
TRAIL OVERPASS
N
W   E
S
Wolf Rd.
River Rd.
Sanders Rd.
Winkleman
294
River Trail Nature Center
?
MATCH LINE

ROUTES

▬▬▬▬	Bicycling Trail
▬ ▬ ▬	Alternate Use Trail
▬▬▬	Roadway

FACILITIES

✛	First Aid
?	Info
P	Parking
禾	Picnic
⌂	Shelter

MILE SCALE

0   1   2

Southern
Section

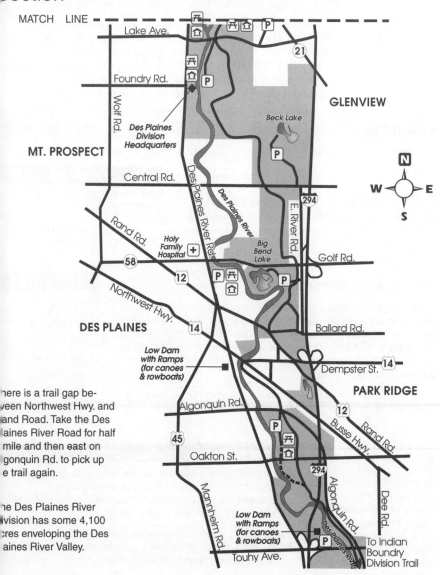

MATCH LINE

Lake Ave.

Wolf Rd.

Foundry Rd.

Des Plaines
Division
Headquarters

MT. PROSPECT

Central Rd.

Rand Rd.

Holy
Family
Hospital

58

Northwest Hwy.

12

DES PLAINES

14

Low Dam
with Ramps
(for canoes
& rowboats)

Algonquin Rd.

45

Oakton St.

Mannheim Rd.

Low Dam
with Ramps
(for canoes
& rowboats)

Touhy Ave.

Des Plaines River Rd.

Des Plaines River

Beck Lake

GLENVIEW

21

E. River Rd.

294

Big
Bend
Lake

Golf Rd.

Ballard Rd.

Dempster St. 14

PARK RIDGE

12

Rand Rd.

Busse Hwy.

294

Dee Rd.

Algonquin Rd.

Des Plaines River

To Indian
Boundry
Division Trail

here is a trail gap be-
ween Northwest Hwy. and
and Road. Take the Des
laines River Road for half
 mile and then east on
gonquin Rd. to pick up
e trail again.

he Des Plaines River
ivision has some 4,100
cres enveloping the Des
aines River Valley.

Des Plaines Division

Des Plaines River Trail

Trail Length	33 miles (49.0 with loops)
Surface	Limestone screenings
Uses	Leisure bicycling, cross country skiing, hiking, horse-back riding (Snowmobiling in northern section only)
Location & Setting	The Des Plaines River Trail parallels its namesake river through Lake County. Open area such as prairies and savannas are common. As you travel through this river valley, look for changes in the landscape. In northern Lake County, the valley is wide and the river meanders. In southern Lake County, the valley is narrow and the river runs a straighter course. Woodlands are more common.
Information	Lake County Forest Preserves (847) 367-6640
County	Lake

Van Patten Woods consists of 972 acres. Enjoy picnic areas, reserveable shelters and shoreline fishing at 74 acre Sterling Lake.

ROUTES

▬▬▬	Bicycling Trail
▬ ▬▬ ▬	Bikeway
▬ ▬▬ ▬	Alternate Bike Trail
= = =	Planned Trail
▬▬▬	Roadway

LAKE COUNTY FOREST PRESERVES

Open daily from 8 am to sunset daily. Alcoholic beverages may not be consumed in or near parking areas. Pets are permitted, except in picnic areas, but must be controlled on a leash (no longer than 10 feet). Forest Preserve Ranger Police regularly patrol the Preserves. Ranger Police receive the same basic training as other Illinois police officers and have the same authority.

More than 23,400 acres make up the Lake County Forest Preserves, a dynamic and unique system of natural and cultural resources.

FACILITIES

?	Info
P	Parking
⚎	Picnic
⓪	Refreshments
⚏	Restrooms
⌂	Shelter
⚐	Water

The southern end of the Des Plaines River Trail currently ends at Hwy. 45 in the Half Day Forest Preserve. Across the river is Wright Woods Forest Preserve. Moving north, the trail passes through MacArthur Woods Forest Preserve in Mettawa, through Old School Forest Preserve, and north almost to the Wisconsin state line.

Right-of-Way Laws

When you come to a stop sign at a two-way stop intersection, remember that the traffic on the cross street has the right-of-way. You must yield the right-of-way to pedestrians and vehicles on the cross street before you go ahead.

Blind, hearing impaired or physically handicapped persons can be identified by their white canes, support or guide dogs. You must always yield the right-of-way to them.

If a policeman directs otherwise, the right-of-way laws do not apply and riders and pedestrians must do as the officer tells them.

Northern Section

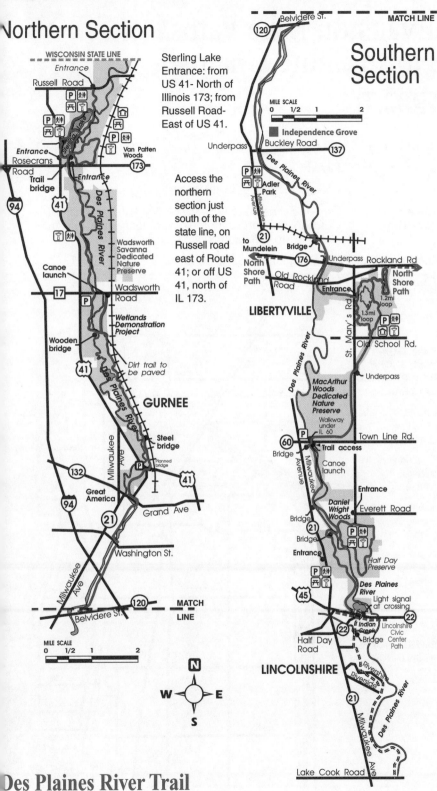

WISCONSIN STATE LINE

Entrance
Russell Road [P] [🚻] [⛺] [🚻]

[P] [🚶] [⛺] [🚻]

Sterling Lake

🏠

[P] [🚻]
[🚻]

Van Patten Woods

Entrance
Rosecrans Road
173

Trail bridge

41

Entrance

94

Des Plaines River

Wadsworth Savanna Dedicated Nature Preserve

Canoe launch

17

[P] Wadsworth Road

Wetlands Demonstration Project

Wooden bridge

41

Dirt trail to be paved

GURNEE

Des Plaines River

Milwaukee Ave.

Steel bridge

132

[P] Planned bridge

Great America

41

94

21

Grand Ave.

Washington St.

Milwaukee Ave.

120   MATCH LINE

Belvidere St.

MILE SCALE
0   1/2   1   2

N
W — E
S

Sterling Lake Entrance: from US 41- North of Illinois 173; from Russell Road- East of US 41.

Access the northern section just south of the state line, on Russell road east of Route 41; or off US 41, north of IL 173.

MATCH LINE

Southern Section

120   Belvidere St.

MILE SCALE
0   1/2   1   2

■ Independence Grove

Underpass   Buckley Road   137

Des Plaines River

[P] [🚻]
[⛺] Adler Park

Milwaukee Avenue

21
to Mundelein   Bridge

176   Underpass   Rockland Rd

North Shore Path   Old Rockland Road   Entrance   North Shore Path

LIBERTYVILLE

1.2mi loop

1.3mi loop   [P] [🚻] 🏠 [⛺]

St. Mary's Rd.

Old School Rd.

Des Plaines River

MacArthur Woods Dedicated Nature Preserve

Underpass

Walkway under IL 60

60   [P]   Town Line Rd.

Bridge   Trail access

Milwaukee Avenue

Canoe launch

Entrance   Everett Road

Daniel Wright Woods

Bridge

21   [P] [🚻] [⛺]

Bridge

Entrance   Half Day Preserve

[P] [🚻] [⛺]

Des Plaines River

45   Light signal at crossing

22

Indian Creek   Lincolnshire Civic Center Path

22   Bridge

Half Day Road

LINCOLNSHIRE

Rivershire

Riverside   Des Plaines River

21

Milwaukee Ave.

Lake Cook Road

Des Plaines River Trail

Evanston Bike Paths/ North Shore Channel

Trail Length	7.0 miles
Surface	Paved
Uses	Leisure bicycling, in-line skating, jogging
Location & Setting	City of Evanston in northeast Cook County north of Chicago and bordering Lake Michigan. Setting is urban, North Shore Channel is open park area.
Information	Evanston Chamber of Commerce (847) 328-1500
County	Cook

EVANSTON-LAKE SHORE PATH TO GREEN BAY TRAIL

Lincoln St. west to Ashland (1 mi.)

Ashland north to Isabella (.4 mi.)

Isabella west to Poplar Dr. (.4 mi.)

Poplar Dr. north to Forest Ave. (1 mi.)

EMERGENCY ASSISTANCE

Dial 911

Fermilab Bike Trail

Trail Length	4.0 miles
Surface	Paved
Uses	Leisure bicycling, cross country skiing, hiking
Location & Setting	The east access is off Batavia Road just west of Hwy. 59. The west access is off Kirk Road about ¾ miles north of Butterfield Road. Tall grass prairie, flood plain woods and wetlands.
Information	Fermilab Prairie Path Volunteers (630) 840-3351
County	DuPage

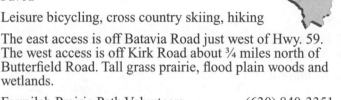

You can learn about everything from subatomic particles to bison at Fermilab. Built in the 1950's, Fermilab is on the cutting edge of particle acceleration research. However, don't miss the woods, ponds, and prairie. The top floor (15th) is open for observation, and can provide a spectacular view of the Fox Valley.

As an alternate, tour the scenic 4 mile trail through Fermilab, or extend it to a 14 mile round trip by way of the Aurora Branch, Batavia Spur and paved paths along Kirk Road and Batavia Road.

FACILITIES

- 🔧 Bike Repair
- 🅿 Parking
- 🚺🚹 Restrooms
- **MF** Multi Facilities Available

Refreshments	First Aid
Telephone	Picnic
Restrooms	Lodging

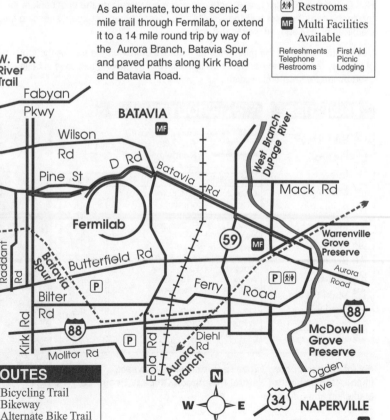

ROUTES

- ──── Bicycling Trail
- ──── Bikeway
- ─ ─ ─ Alternate Bike Trail
- ──── Roadway

Fox River Trail

Trail Length	41.7 miles	
Surface	Paved, limestone screenings	
Uses	Leisure bicycling, cross country skiing, hiking	
Location & Setting	Follows the Fox River between Crystal Lake and Aurora. Open spaces and small communities.	
Information	Fox Valley Park District	(630) 232-5980
	Dundee Township Tourist Center	(847) 426-2255
County	McHenry, Kane	

This trail winds through the Fox River Valley running northward from Aurora to Crystal Lake. You'll bike through forest and nature preserves, and several historic and interesting communities. This popular trail connects to the Illinois Prairie Path to the east, to the Great Western Trail west of St. Charles and to the Virgil Gilman Trail in Aurora. Plans include extending the trail via bike-ways through Crystal Lake, then connecting to the Prairie Trail (north section) which will continue to the Wisconsin state line.

Red Oak Nature Center is a 40 acre oak and maple forest on the east bank of the Fox River. Inside the nature center building, you'll find a contemporary museum stressing the four basic elements of life...sun, air, water and soil.

Devil's Cave is one of the most unusual natural features on the trail. Although small, this is one of the very few caves in northeastern Illinois. Rich in folklore, this cave is believed to have been used by the Pottawatomie Indians.

FACILITIES

- 🔧 Bike Repair
- ➕ First Aid
- ❓ Info
- 🏨 Lodging
- 🅿 Parking
- 🍴 Picnic
- 🍽 Refreshments
- 🚻 Restrooms
- 🏠 Shelter
- **MF** Multi Facilities Available

Refreshments	First Aid
Telephone	Picnic
Restrooms	Lodging

ROUTES

▬▬▬	Bicycling Trail
▬ ▬ ▬	Alternate Bike Trail
▬▬▬	Roadway

ROUTE SLIP	SEGMENT	TOTAL
Crystal Lk. Ave. (Crystal Lake)		
Hwy. 62 (Algonquin)	4.0	41.7
Bolz Rd. (Carpentersville)	3.0	37.7
Hwy. 72/68 (E. Dundee)	4.0	34.7
Hwy. 90 (Elgin)	3.5	30.7
Hwy. 20 (Elgin)	5.1	27.2
River Crossing (S. Elgin)	2.9	22.1
Black Hawk Forest Pres.	2.2	19.2
Army Trail Rd. (St. Chas.)	2.5	17.0
Main St. (St. Charles)	3.0	14.5
State St. (Geneva)	2.0	11.5
Fabyan Pkwy. (Batavia)	1.5	9.5
Wilson St. (Batavia)	1.0	8.0
Hwy. 88	5.0	7.0
New York St. (Aurora)	2.0	2.0

For information concerning trail activities, please contact:
Illinois Department of Natural Resources Office of Resource
Marketing and Education
524 S. Second St.
Springfield, IL 62701-1787
217/782-7454

Northern Section

(176)

CRYSTAL LAKE
➕ P MF

Crystal Lake Ave.

MILE SCALE
0   1   2   3

Pyott Rd.
Virginia Rd.
(31)
4.0 mi
(14)
Fox River

🔧

BARRINGTON
🔧 ➕

ALGONQUIN
MF
?
🔧

3.0 mi

(62)
Lake Cook Rd.

MCHENRY COUNTY
KANE COUNTY

P 🚻
Buffalo Park
Forest Preserve

Bolz Rd.

Fox River Shores
Forest Preserve
P 🚻

(25)

4.0 mi

CARPENTERSVILLE

WEST DUNDEE
MF

(68)
🔧 P

MF

(72)

3.5 mi

EAST DUNDEE

Voyageurs Landing
Forest Preserve
P 🚻

P 🚻
Tyler Creek
Forest Preserve

🔧
(90)

6.1 mi

ELGIN
P
MF
MF 🔧

🔧
P

(20)

2.9 mi
(25)
MF 🔧
SOUTH ELGIN

Fox River

Prairie Path

MATCH LINE

Southern Section

MATCH LINE

2.2 mi
Blackhawk
Forest Preserve
MF

Trolley Museum
Fox River
Prairie Path
(25)

Teckawitha
Environmental
Center

(31)
(25)
Army Trail Rd.

5.7 mi

River Bluff
Forest Preserve
P 🚻

Leory
Oakes
Forest
Preserve

Pottawatomie
Park
P

Main St.
(64)

to the
Great
Western
Trail

(31)

ST. CHARLES

P

MF

P 🚻 🔧
State St.

(38)
GENEVA

4.5
mi

MF

Fabyan
Forest Preserve
P 🚻 🛉

P
Fabyan Pkwy.

Red Oak
Trail (east
side of river)
4.5 mi

Wilson St.

BATAVIA MF
🍴 P

?
P

Red Oak
Nature
Center

Glenwood Park
Forest Preserve
P 🚻

(56)
Butterfield Rd.

5.0 mi
Les
Arends
Forest
Preserve

**NORTH
AURORA**
(31)

P 🚻
Devil's
Cave

(88)
Prairie
Path

MF

2.0
mi
McCullough
Park

Prairie
Path

➕ P
Illinois Ave.
P

to Virgil
Gilman
Trail

(31)
Galena
Blvd.

Fox River
(25)
AURORA

MF
N
(30)
W   E
S

MILE SCALE
0   1   2   3

Fox River Trail

55

Fullersburg Forest Preserve

Trail Length	2.5 miles of bicycling trails, 3.25 miles total
Surface	Screenings, Asphalt
Uses	Leisure bicycling, cross country skiing, hiking/jogging, horseback riding
Location & Setting	Located between Oak Brook and Hinsdale in east central DuPage County, Fullersburg Forest Preserve can be accessed from Spring Road, ½ mile northwest of York Road Woodlands, prairie, creek crossings.
Information	Forest Preserve District of DuPage County (630) 790-4900
County	Du Page

Fullersburg Woods, with 221 acres, is a nature sanctuary for plants and animals. It has a Visitors and Environmental Center which is open daily from 9am to 5pm.

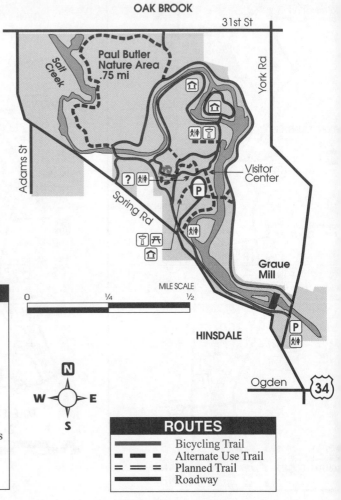

FACILITIES

- ✚ First Aid
- ? Info
- P Parking
- 🎋 Picnic
- 🚻 Restrooms
- 🏠 Shelter
- 🚰 Water
- **MF** Multi Facilities Available

Refreshments	First Aid
Telephone	Picnic
Restrooms	Lodging

ROUTES

———	Bicycling Trail
– – –	Alternate Use Trail
= = =	Planned Trail
▬▬▬	Roadway

Fulton Bike Trail (F.A.S.T.)

Trail Length	6 miles existing, 8+ miles planned	
Surface	Asphalt, shared streets	
Uses	Leisure bicycling, in-line skating, cross country skiing, hiking	
Location & Setting	Located in Fulton along the Mississippi River in northwest Illinois. Setting is riverfront, city streets.	
Information	Fulton Chamber of Commerce P.O. Box 253 Fulton, IL 61252	
County	Whiteside	

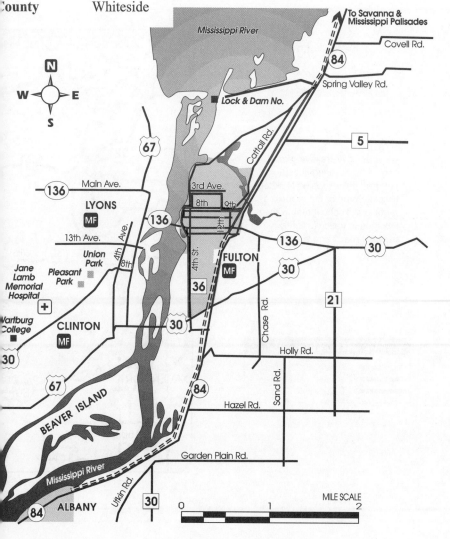

Grand Illinois Trail

Trail Length	475 miles
Location & Setting	Existing and planned trails forming a loop of northern Illinois, from the suburbs of Chicago to the Mississippi and from the Wisconsin border to the I & M Canal.
Information	Illinois Department of Conservation (217) 782-3715 Illinois Trails Conservancy (815) 569-2472
County	Covers 16 counties

A series of 17 trails and road segments covering several hundred miles looping Northern Illinois. Some of the proposed route is still conceptual, with linkages to trails via lightly traveled roads and streets.

ROUTES

Bicycling Trail
Bikeway Incomplete
Roadway

GRAND ILLINOIS TRAIL SYSTEM SEGMENTS

1. Local roads
2. Pecatonica Trail
3. Rockford Area Trails
4. Stone Bridge and Long Prairie Trails
5. Conceptual connection
6. Crystal Lake/Harvard Trail segment
7. Prairie Trail segment
8. Fox River Trail segment
9. Illinois Prairie Path segment
10. Des Plaines River Trail segment
11. Centennial Trail
12. Lockport Historical & Joliet Heritage Trails (& roads)
13. Illinois and Michigan (I & M) Canal State Trail segment
14. Conceptual connection
15. Hennepin Canal State Trail segment
16. Conceptual connection
17. Great River Trail

Grand Illinois Trail

Grant Woods Forest Preserve

Trail Length   3.3 miles

Surface   Limestone screenings

Uses   Leisure bicycling, cross country skiing, jogging, snowmobiling

Location & Setting   Grant Woods is east of Fox Lake and bounded by Rte. 59 on the west, Rte. 83 on the east, Rte. 132 north and Rte. 134 south. Enter on Monaville Rd. east of Rte. 59. The northern half is largely marsh and prairie.

Information   Lake County Forest Preserve   (847) 367-6640

County   Lake

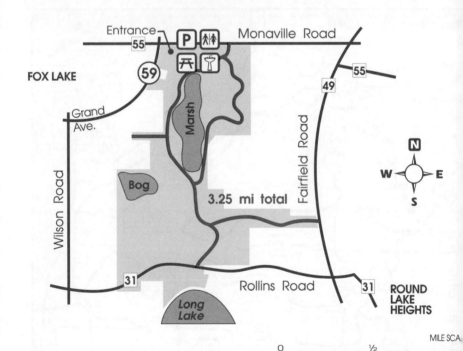

FACILITIES

- **P** Parking
- **⊼** Picnic
- **⋔⋔** Restrooms
- **☂** Water

ROUTES

Bicycling Trail
Roadway

Great Western Trail

Trail Length	18 miles
Surface	Limestone screenings
Uses	Leisure bicycling, cross country skiing, hiking/ jogging, snowmobiling
Location & Setting	This 18 mile trail extends from the LeRoy Oakes Forest Preserve west of St. Charles to Sycamore at Old State and Airport Road in Kane and DeKalb counties and stands on the former site of the Chicago and Northwestern Railroad line. Rural landscape, wetlands, farmlands, small communities.
Information	Kane County Forest Preserve (630) 232-5980
County	DeKalb, Kane

There is a bike route from the city of DeKalb to a nature trail. The Peace Road Trail links DeKalb and Sycamore with a recreational path.

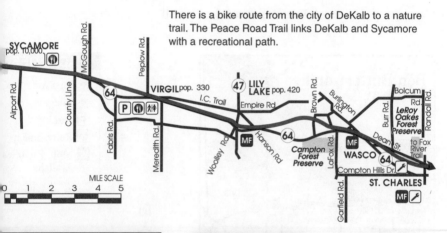

ROUTES

Bicycling Trail
Roadway

There are plans to provide a 3.5 mile corridor between the Fox River Trail and the Great Western Trail. The path will run south from Silver Glen Road along Randall Road on a county highway easement to LeRoy Oakes Forest Preserve, where it will connect with the Great Western Trail.

FACILITIES

Bike Repair	
?	Info
Lodging	
P	Parking
Picnic	
Refreshments	
Restrooms	
MF	Multi Facilities Available

Refreshments	First Aid
Telephone	Picnic
Restrooms	Lodging

The Great Western Trail is a rail-to-trails conversion. Horseback riding is permitted from Lily Lake to LeRoy Oakes. Snowmobiling is permitted with 4 or more inches of snow.

Great River Trail
Ben Butterworth Pathway

Trail Length	62.0 miles
Surface	Paved paths (10 feet), shared streets, undeveloped
Uses	Leisure bicycling, in-line skating, cross country skiing, hiking/jogging
Location & Setting	The Great River Trail will eventually run from Rock Island to the Mississippi Palisades State Park, north of Savanna, along the Mississippi River in northwest Illinois. The setting is riverfront, urban to small communities, rural, woods, open areas, farmland.
Information	Bi-State Regional Commission (309) 793-6300 Parks & Recreation Dept. (309) 752-1573 Hampton Village Hall (309) 755-7165
County	Rock Island, Whiteside, Carroll

FACILITIES

- ✚ First Aid
- 🛏 Lodging
- Ⓟ Parking
- 🔟 Refreshments
- **MF** Multi Facilities Available

Refreshments   First Aid
Telephone   Picnic
Restrooms   Lodging

MILE SCALE
0   5   10   15   20

Always lock your bicycle when it is parked. Register your bicycle with your local police department if possible. Be sure to keep your bike's serial number in a safe place.

If you are uncertain of the condition of your bicycle, visit a local bike shop. Most shops offer free safety inspections and books on do-it-yourself maintenance.

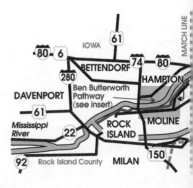

Trailheads

Rock Island	Sunset Park, 18th Avenue and IL Route 92
East Moline	Waterfront & Mississippi Parks (north sides of city)
Hampton	Riverfront Park (south side), Illiniwek Park (north side)
Rapids City	Shuler's Shady Grove Park
Port Byron	Boat access area
Albany	Boat access area
Thomson	Downtown area, Thomson Causeway, Buck's Barn
Savanna	Downtown area
Mississippi Palisades State Park	

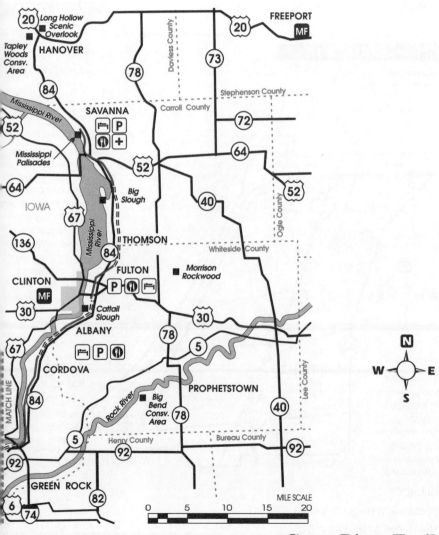

Great River Trail

Green Bay Trail

Trail Length	6.0 miles
Surface	Paved
Uses	Leisure bicycling, cross country skiing, hiking
Location & Setting	From Wilmette to the Lake County line, running mostly parallel to the Chicago and Northwestern rail line. Urban setting.
Information	Winnetka Park District (847) 501-2040
County	Cook

FACILITIES

🔧 Bike Repair
P Parking
MF Multi Facilities Available

Refreshments   First Aid
Telephone   Picnic
Restrooms   Lodging

ROUTES

━━━ Bicycling Trail
━━━ Roadway

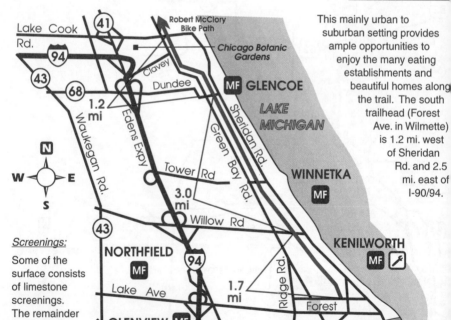

This mainly urban to suburban setting provides ample opportunities to enjoy the many eating establishments and beautiful homes along the trail. The south trailhead (Forest Ave. in Wilmette) is 1.2 mi. west of Sheridan Rd. and 2.5 mi. east of I-90/94.

Screenings:

Some of the surface consists of limestone screenings. The remainder is paved, or street/sidewalk connections.

GLENCOE

- Scott Ave. & Harbor St. (.4 mi.)
- South Ave. & Hazel Ave. (.2 mi.)
- Maple Hill Rd. & Ravinia Park (1.1 mi.)

MILE SCALE

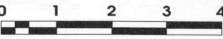

0   1   2   3   4

Green Belt Forest Preserve

Trail Length	Approximately 4 miles, 5 miles of looped trails
Surface	Crushed gravel
Uses	Leisure bicycling, cross country skiing, hiking
Location Setting	The Greenbelt Forest Preserve is nestled between the cities of Waukegan and North Chicago, east of Route 41 and south of Route 120.
Information	Lake County Forest Preserve
County	Lake

(847) 367-6640

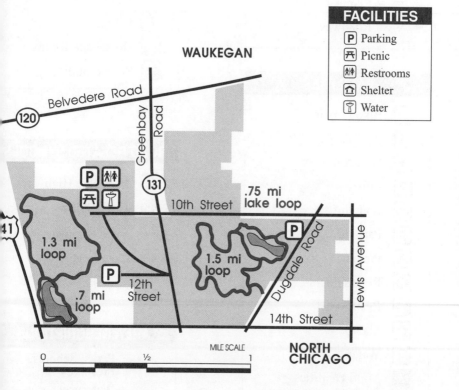

FACILITIES

- **P** Parking
- 🏕 Picnic
- 🚻 Restrooms
- 🏠 Shelter
- 🚰 Water

WAUKEGAN

Belvedere Road

120

Greenbay Road

131

10th Street

.75 mi lake loop

1.3 mi loop

41

1.5 mi loop

P

Dugdale Road

Lewis Avenue

P

12th Street

.7 mi loop

14th Street

MILE SCALE

0   ½   1

NORTH CHICAGO

Entrances- West Section: off Green Bay Road (Route 131) 12th Street (open May - Nov) East Section: Dugdale Road, south of 10th Street (open year round)

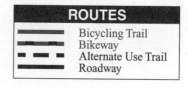

ROUTES

- Bicycling Trail
- Bikeway
- Alternate Use Trail
- Roadway

Explanation of Symbols

ROUTES

- ———— Biking Trail
- ▬▬▬ Bikeway
- ▬ ▬ ▬ Alternate Bike Trail
- ▬ ▬ ▬ Alternate Use Trail
- = = = Planned Trail
- ▬▬▬ Roadway

FACILITIES

- Bike Repair
- Camping
- First Aid
- Info
- Lodging
- Parking
- Picnic
- Refreshments
- Restrooms
- Shelter
- Water
- MF Multi Facilities Available

Refreshments	First Aid
Telephone	Picnic
Restrooms	Lodging

TRAIL USES

- Mountain Biking
- Leisure Biking
- In Line Skating
- (X-C) Cross-Country Skiing
- Hiking
- Horseback Riding
- Snowmobiling

ROAD RELATED SYMBOLS

- (45) Interstate Highway
- (45) U.S. Highway
- (45) State Highway
- 45 County Highway

AREA DESCRIPTIONS

- Parks, Schools, Preserves, etc.
- Waterway
- Mileage Scale
- Directional

Greene Valley Forest Preserve

Trail Length	6.2 miles
Surface	Gravel, mowed turf
Uses	Fat tire bicycling, cross country skiing, hiking, horseback riding
Location & Setting	Greene Valley Forest Preserve is located in far south central DuPage County, on Greene Road, ½ mile south of 75th Street. 1,400 acres of woodlands and grasslands.
Information	Forest Preserve District of DuPage County (630) 790-4900
County	DuPage

Trails are symbol coded and may be traveled in both directions. Loop trails range from 1.75 to 6.25 miles.

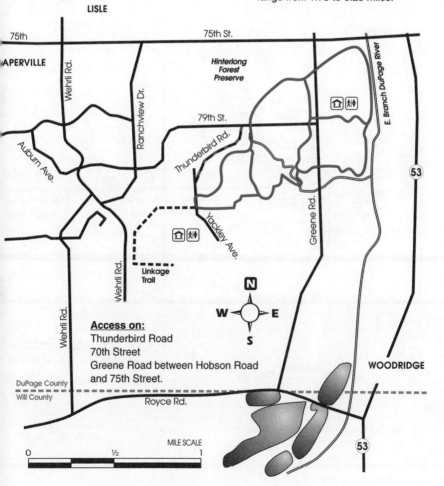

Heartland Pathways

Trail Length	31 miles
Surface	Ballast
Uses	Fat tire bicycling, hiking
Location & Setting	An abandoned railbed that runs from Clinton to Seymour in east central Illinois. Its 100 foot wide corridor contains one of the last remnants of tall grass prairies in Illinois.
Information	Heartland Pathways (217) 351-1911
County	DeWitt, Pratt, Champaign

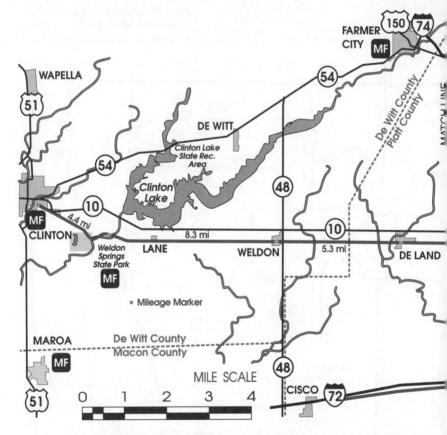

Access can be achieved at connecting
roads. There is no designated parking.

FACILITIES

+ First Aid

MF Multi Facilities
   Available

Refreshments   First Aid
Telephone   Picnic
Restrooms   Lodging

The Heartland Pathways promotes
the observation and conservation
of the natural and cultural
landscapes of Illinois.

ROUTES

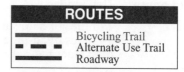

Bicycling Trail
Alternate Use Trail
Roadway

Points of interests include a
railroad museum in Monticello and
the Allerton Park country estate
with its formal gardens, statuary,
pools and hiking trails, just west of
Monticello.

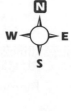

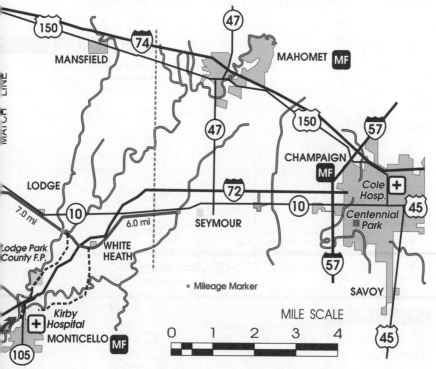

Hennepin Canal Parkway

Trail Length	104.5 miles
Surface	17 miles of hard surface; 3 miles oil & chip; 14 miles of ad-lime from Lock 33 to Route 92; remainder mowed.
Uses	Fat tire bicycling, cross country skiing, hiking, horseback riding (except from Bridge 43 to 45).
Location & Setting	The Hennepin Canal Parkway is a unique linear waterway corridor in northwestern Illinois. The main line of the waterway extends from the great bend of the Illinois River to the Mississippi River, west of Milan.
Information	Illinois Dept. of Conservation Site Superintendant 815/454-2328
County	Bureau, Henry, Lee Rock Island, Whiteside.

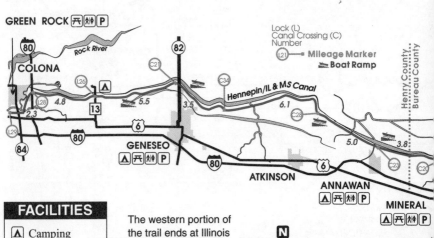

FACILITIES

- 🅰 Camping
- 🅿 Parking
- 🌲 Picnic
- 🚻 Restrooms
- **MF** Multi Facilities Available

Refreshments   First Aid
Telephone   Picnic
Restrooms   Lodging

The western portion of the trail ends at Illinois Route 82 north of Genesseo.

There are 33 locks on the canal. The canal was completed in 1907, but was only used for a short while before being replaced by the railroad.

The parkway is a popular recreatonal area for pleasure boating, picnicking, primitive camping, horseback riding, snowmobiling, backpacking, and hiking in addition to bicycling. A feeder from the Rock River connects to the main line between Sheffield and Mineral. There are numerous parking areas and road accesses along the parkway.

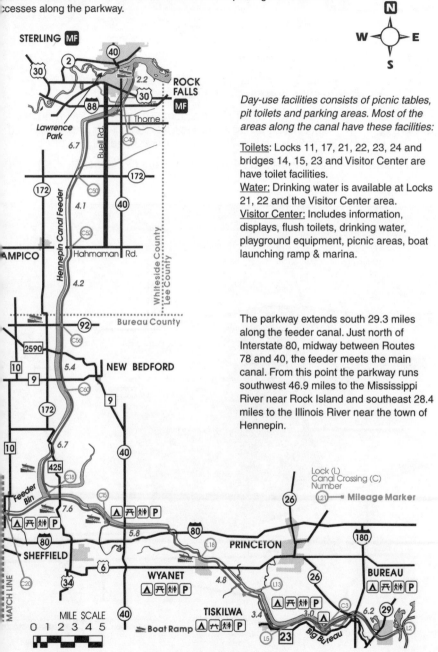

Day-use facilities consists of picnic tables, pit toilets and parking areas. Most of the areas along the canal have these facilities:

Toilets: Locks 11, 17, 21, 22, 23, 24 and bridges 14, 15, 23 and Visitor Center are have toilet facilities.
Water: Drinking water is available at Locks 21, 22 and the Visitor Center area.
Visitor Center: Includes information, displays, flush toilets, drinking water, playground equipment, picnic areas, boat launching ramp & marina.

The parkway extends south 29.3 miles along the feeder canal. Just north of Interstate 80, midway between Routes 78 and 40, the feeder meets the main canal. From this point the parkway runs southwest 46.9 miles to the Mississippi River near Rock Island and southeast 28.4 miles to the Illinois River near the town of Hennepin.

Hennepin Canal Parkway

Herrick Lake Forest Preserve

Trail Length	4.0 miles
Surface	Limestone screenings
Uses	Leisure bicycling, cross country skiing, hiking/jogging, horseback riding.
Location & Setting	Located in central DuPage County, between Winfield and Naperville. Access from Herrick Road or Butterfield Road. Herrick Lake has 760 acres with a 21 acre lake.
Information	Forest Preserve District of DuPage County (630) 790-4900
County	DuPage

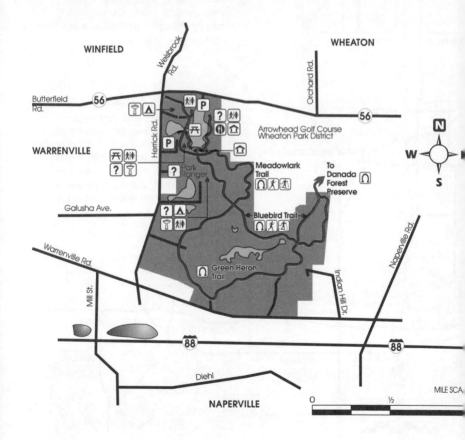

There is a concession building on the eastern shore of the lake. Canoes and row boats are available for rental.

Hononegah Recreation Path

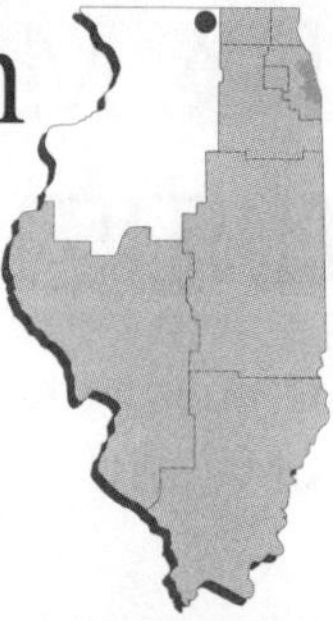

Trail Length	2.5 miles
Surface	Asphalt
Uses	Leisure bicycling, in-line skating, hiking
Location & Setting	The path runs along the south side of Hononegah Road between Hwy. 251 and proceeds northwest ¼ mile west of Route 2. Open area with small communities at either end.
Information	Rockford Park District (815) 987-8865
County	Winnebago

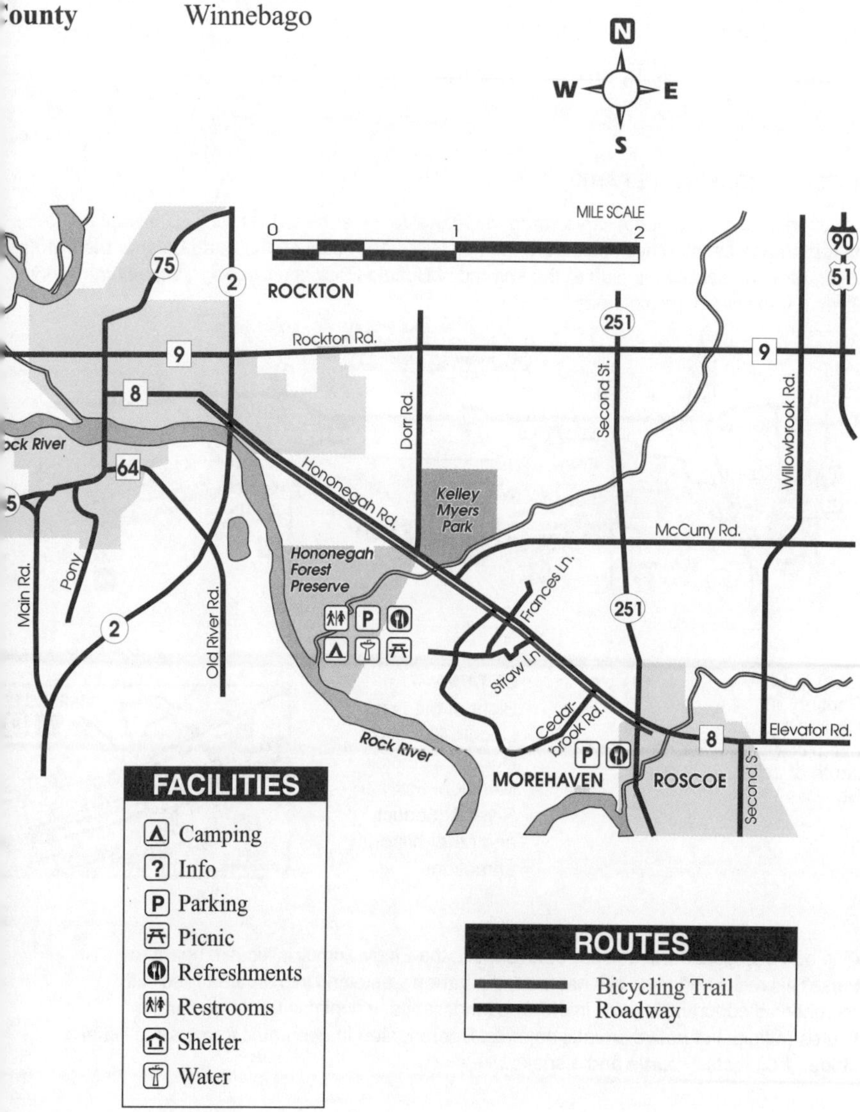

FACILITIES

- **A** Camping
- **?** Info
- **P** Parking
- **☶** Picnic
- **◑** Refreshments
- **⚇** Restrooms
- **⌂** Shelter
- **☟** Water

ROUTES

- ▬▬▬ Bicycling Trail
- ▬▬▬ Roadway

I & M Canal State Trail

Trail Length	56 miles
Surface	Limestone screenings
Uses	Leisure bicycling, cross country skiing, hiking, snowmobiling
Location & Setting	In northeast Illinois, the eastern trailhead begins at the Channanon access. The trail proceeds west to the city of LaSalle, where there are multiple access points and parking Rural landscape, prairie, small communities
Information	I & M Canal State Trail (815) 942-9501
County	Will, Grundy, LaSalle

BUFFALO ROCK STATE PARK

Directions: Boyce Memorial Drive south to Ottawa Avenue. West 1.8 miles, past Naplate, to the park entrance. Located five miles from the Fox River Aqueduct on the north bank of the Illinois River. Atop the sandstone bluff at the summit of Buffalo Rock is a sweeping view of the Illinois River. It has several picnic areas

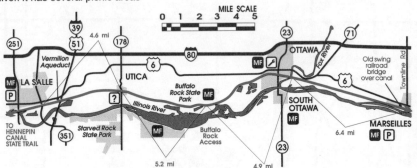

LA SALLE—
Parking off Canal St. one half block south of Joliet St.

OTTAWA—
Sight of the first Lincoln-Douglas Debate, Reddick Mansion, Fox River Aqueduct and other historic attractions.

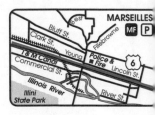

One of the largest earth sculptures ever built, the Effigy Tumuli is located near the park. This reclaimed mine site has turned a barren wasteland into an area filled with recreational opportunities and interesting landscapes. It contains five large earthen figures (effigies) of native aquatic animals. Represented in geometric forms are a water strider, frog, catfish, turtle and a snake.

Bicyclists can take advantage of the groomed towpath to enjoy the natural and manmade wonders. The trail is marked and has various wayside exhibits that describe features of the canal era.

The I&M (Illinois and Michigan) Canal provided the first complete water route from the east coast to the Gulf of Mexico by connecting Lake Michigan to the Mississippi River by way of the Illinois River.

FACILITIES

- 🔧 Bike Repair
- ❓ Info
- 🅿 Parking
- **MF** Multi Facilities Available

Refreshments   First Aid
Telephone   Picnic
Restrooms   Lodging

CHANNANON ACCESS—
Exit Hwy. 6 at Canal St. Proceed one half mile southeast to Story St., then one block west.

AUX SABLE—
This access area is eight miles from Channahon where an aqueduct, lock and locktender's house can be found.

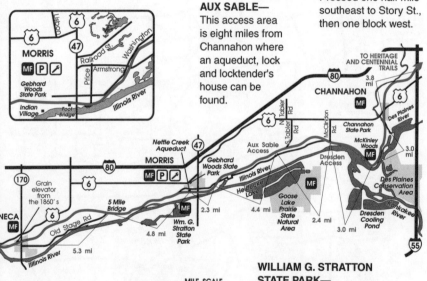

MILE SCALE
0 1 2 3 4 5

WILLIAM G. STRATTON STATE PARK—
Located in Morris, it provides public boat access to the Illinois River. Picnicking and fishing are popular here.

GEBHARD WOODS STATE PARK—
Thirty acres of slightly rolling terrain dotted with many stately shade trees.

ROUTES

━━━ Bicycling Trail
━━━ Roadway

I & M Canal State Trail

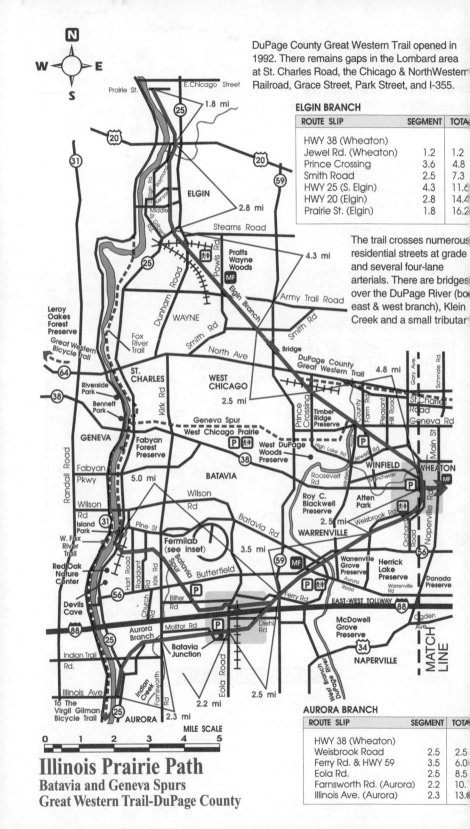

DuPage County Great Western Trail opened in 1992. There remains gaps in the Lombard area at St. Charles Road, the Chicago & NorthWestern Railroad, Grace Street, Park Street, and I-355.

ELGIN BRANCH

ROUTE SLIP	SEGMENT	TOTA
HWY 38 (Wheaton)		
Jewel Rd. (Wheaton)	1.2	1.2
Prince Crossing	3.6	4.8
Smith Road	2.5	7.3
HWY 25 (S. Elgin)	4.3	11.6
HWY 20 (Elgin)	2.8	14.4
Prairie St. (Elgin)	1.8	16.2

The trail crosses numerous residential streets at grade and several four-lane arterials. There are bridges over the DuPage River (both east & west branch), Klein Creek and a small tributar

Illinois Prairie Path
Batavia and Geneva Spurs
Great Western Trail-DuPage County

AURORA BRANCH

ROUTE SLIP	SEGMENT	TOTA
HWY 38 (Wheaton)		
Weisbrook Road	2.5	2.5
Ferry Rd. & HWY 59	3.5	6.0
Eola Rd.	2.5	8.5
Farnsworth Rd. (Aurora)	2.2	10.
Illinois Ave. (Aurora)	2.3	13.0

Illinois Prairie Path
Batavia and Geneva Spurs
Great Western Trail-DuPage County

Trail Length	Illinois Prairie Path	44.2 miles
	Batavia Spur	5.0 miles
	Geneva Spur	5.0 miles
	Great Western Trail	11.4 miles
Surface	Limestone screenings (Batavia Spur is partially paved)	
Uses	Leisure bicycling, cross country skiing, hiking/jogging (horseback riding limited)	
Location & Setting	Refer to route slips for location of trails. Prairie, wetlands, open spaces, woods, urban communities.	
Information	The Illinois Prairie Path	(630) 665-5310
County	Cook, DuPage, Kane	

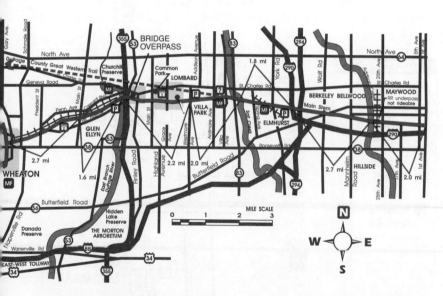

Along much of The Illinois Prairie Path, nature is abundant. Pheasants, flickers, robins, cardinals, chickadees and goldfinch can be found. Many different species of plants are found throughout the seasons. During spring look for mayapples, which look like small green umbrellas popping out of the ground. In summer, violets and onions are in bloom. Autumn brings out goldenrod and asters.

THE ILLINOIS PRAIRIE PATH MAIN STEM

ROUTE SLIP	SEGMENT	TOTAL
HWY 38 (Wheaton)		
Main St. (Glen Ellyn)	2.7	2.7
Du Page River (E. Branch)	1.6	4.3
Westmore Ave. (Lombard)	2.2	6.5
Salt Creek	2.0	8.5
HWY 290 (Elmhurst)	1.8	10.3
Addison Creek	2.7	13.0
First Ave. (Maywood)	2.0	15.0

Illinois Beach State Park

Trail Length	8 miles	
Surface	Limestone screenings, packed earth	
Uses	Leisure bicycling, cross country skiing, hiking/jogging	
Location & Setting	Parallels the Lake Michigan shoreline from south of Zion to the Wisconsin State line. Separating the Northern and Southern Units is Commonwealth Edison's power plant. The Northern unit includes the North Point Marina. Additional trail development is planned.	
	Northern Unit—The path runs from the Marina to San Pond and to the railroad tracks near 7th St. in Winthrop Harbor. *Southern Unit* —The path extends along 29th Street to connect to the Zion Bikeway.	
Information	Zion Beach State Park	(847) 662-4811
County	Lake	

FACILITIES

- 🅰 Camping
- ? Info
- 🅿 Parking
- 🍴 Picnic
- 🚻 Restrooms
- 🏠 Shelter
- 💧 Water
- **MF** Multi Facilities Available

Refreshments   First Aid
Telephone   Picnic
Restrooms   Lodging

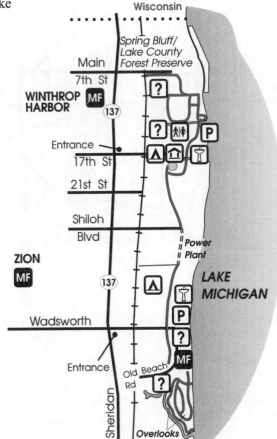

Independence Grove

Trail Length	7 miles
Surface	Paved, crushed limestone
Uses	Leisure bicycling, cross-country skiing, hiking
Location & Setting	A 7-mile trail system located off Rte 137 in north Libertyville. There is both a paved and a crushed stone trail overlooking and circling a 115-acre lake. Facilities include bicycle & boat rental, water, restrooms, picnic area and a Visitors Center. Opened in 2001.
Information	Lake County Forest Preserve (847) 367-6640
County	Lake

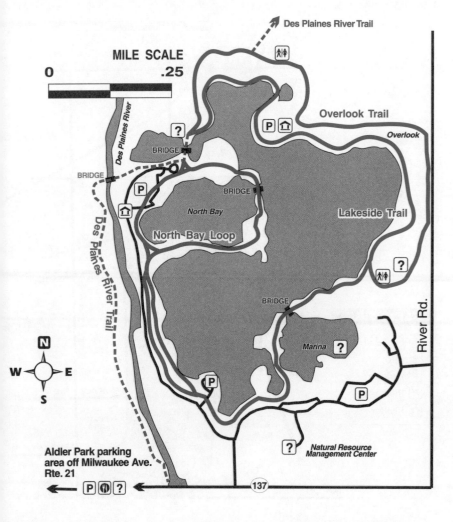

Indian Boundry Division

Trail Length	10 .8 miles
Surface	Natural groomed
Uses	Fat tire bicycling, hiking, horseback riding
Location & Setting	Located along the east bank of the Des Plaines River in northwest Cook County. The trail begins at Madison Street, east of First Avenue in Maywood, and follows the Des Plaines River north to Touhy Avenue, east of the Tri-State Tollway in Des Plaines.
Information	Emergency Assistance 911
	Cook County Forest Preserve District (708) 366-9420
County	Cook

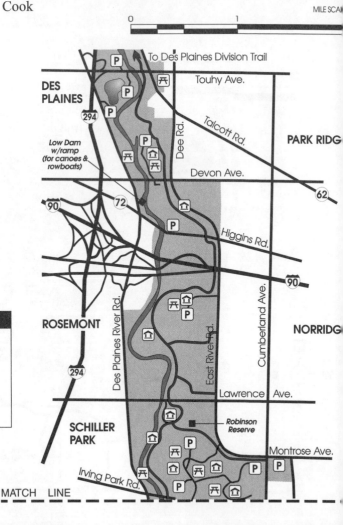

FACILITIES

- ✚ First Aid
- ? Info
- P Parking
- 🎋 Picnic
- 🏠 Shelter

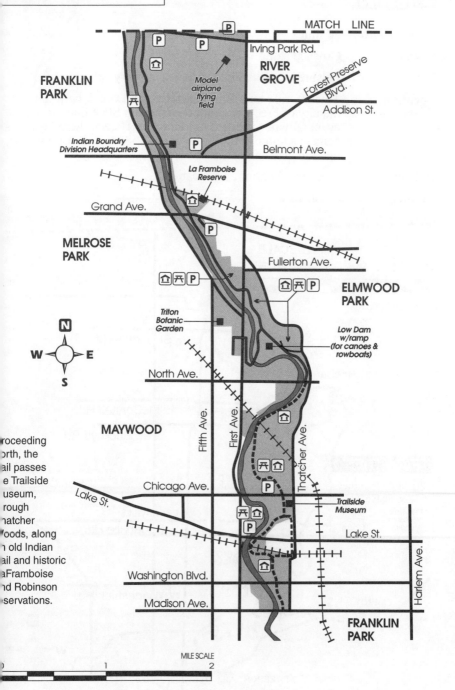

ROUTES

ROUTES

- ▬▬▬ Bicycling Trail
- ▬ ▬ ▬ Alternate Use Trail
- ▬▬▬ Roadway

The trail connects to the Salt Creek Forest Preserve to the south and to the Des Plaines River Division to the north.

MATCH LINE

Irving Park Rd.

RIVER GROVE

Forest Preserve Blvd.

Addison St.

FRANKLIN PARK

Model airplane flying field

Indian Boundry Division Headquarters

Belmont Ave.

La Framboise Reserve

Grand Ave.

MELROSE PARK

Fullerton Ave.

ELMWOOD PARK

Triton Botanic Garden

Low Dam w/ramp (for canoes & rowboats)

North Ave.

Fifth Ave.

First Ave.

MAYWOOD

Thatcher Ave.

Chicago Ave.

Lake St.

Trailside Museum

Lake St.

Harlem Ave.

Washington Blvd.

Madison Ave.

FRANKLIN PARK

N W E S

Proceeding north, the trail passes the Trailside Museum, through Thatcher Woods, along an old Indian trail and historic LaFramboise and Robinson Reservations.

MILE SCALE
0   1   2

Indian Boundry Division

81

Jane Adams Trail

Trail Length	20 miles
Surface	Crushed stone
Uses	Leisure bicycling, hiking, cross-country skiing
Location & Setting	This 20-mile trail runs along Richland Creek between the city of Freeport and the Wisconsin State line. It will eventually be extended to Madison. The southern terminus connects to the Grand Illinois Trail. Setting is rolling hills, open fields and farmland.
Information	Freeport Economic Foundation (815) 756-1350
County	Stephenson

Wisconsin State Line

MILE SCALE

0   1   2   3   4   5

26

Henderson Rd.

4

ORANGEVILLE

W. St. James Rd.

MCCONNELL

Grand
Illinois
Trail

BUENA
VISTA

19   E. McConnell Rd.

W. Buckeye Rd.

FACILITIES

MF Multi Facilities
   Available

Refreshments   First Aid
Telephone   Picnic
Restrooms   Lodging

RED
OAK

Cedarville/Dakota Trail

CEDARVILLE

5   E. Cedarville Rd.

75

SCIOTO
MILLS

ELEROY

23

W. Winneshiek Rd.

20   20W

26

20

N
W   E
S

FREEPORT MF

75

Jubilee College State Park

Trail Length	15 miles
Surface	Natural – groomed
Uses	Fat tire bicycling, hiking, horseback riding, snowmobiling
Location & Setting	Jubilee College State Park is located about 10-miles northwest of Peoria between the towns of Kickapoo and Brimfield. The Park offers some 15-miles of mountain bike trails, and is open to horseback riding and snowmobiling. Setting is rolling terrain and open prairie.
Information	Jubilee College State Park (309) 446-3758
County	Peoria

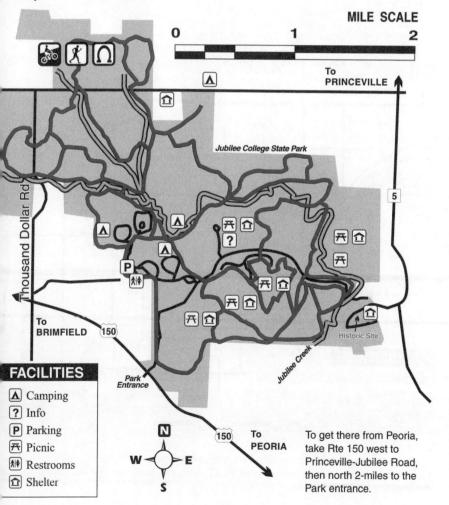

FACILITIES

- Ⓐ Camping
- ? Info
- Ⓟ Parking
- 🎪 Picnic
- 🚻 Restrooms
- ⌂ Shelter

To get there from Peoria, take Rte 150 west to Princeville-Jubilee Road, then north 2-miles to the Park entrance.

Kankakee River State Park

Trail Length	8 miles
Surface	Crushed Limestone
Uses	Leisure bicycling, fat tire bicycling, cross country skiing, hiking, horseback riding
Location & Setting	Located about 8 miles northwest of Kankakee in northeast Illinois. The park consists of some 4,000 acres with Routes 102 on the north and 113 on the south. Both I- 55 and I-57 provide convenient accesses. Straddles the Kankakee River - bluffs, canyons, heavy woods.
Information	Kankakee River State Park (815) 933-1383
County	Will

The bicycle trails begins at Davis Creek Area and travels to the Chippewa Campground. At one point it crosses a suspension bridge. There are 12 miles of cross country ski trails, and a 3 mile hiking trail with views of limestone canyons and a frothy waterfall. There is also a 12 mile equestrian trail.

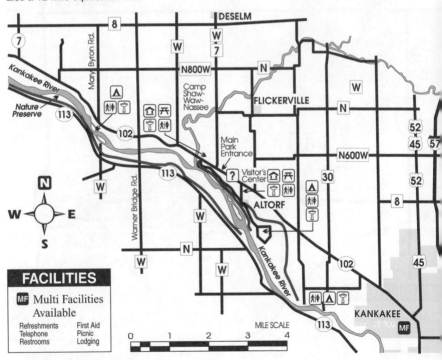

Canoe rentals are available at Bird Park in Kankakee (815) 932-6555. It's a four to six hour trip the park from there. There is a concession stand, camping and picnicking areas. Bicycle rentals are available (815/932-3337).

Kickapoo State Park

Trail Length	16 miles (loops)
Surface	Natural - groomed
Uses	Fat tire bicycling (difficult), cross country skiing, hiking
Location & Setting	Located in east central Illinois, 10 miles west of Indiana and 35 miles east of Champaign/Urbana. Kickapoo State Park consists of 2,842 acres and has 22 deep water ponds. The setting is made up of lushly forested uplands and bottomlands along the Middle Fork of the Vermilion River. There is easy access from I-74 and connecting roads surrounding the park.
Information	Kickapoo State Park (717) 442-4915
County	Vermilion

Kickapoo owes its crystal clear pond and forested ridges to the regenerative powers of nature, which reclaimed the area over the past 50 years after a century of strip mining.

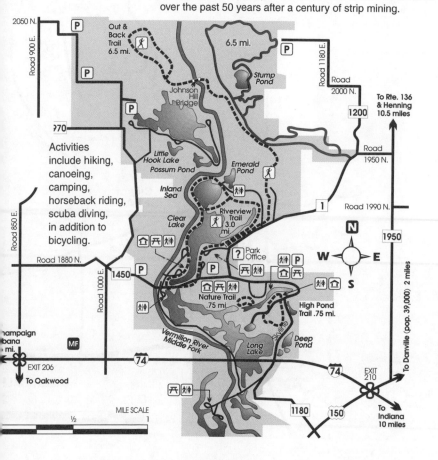

Kishwaukee Kiwanis Pathway

Trail Length	6.5 miles
Surface	Paved
Uses	Leisure bicycling, hiking, cross-country skiing
Location & Setting	The Kishwaukee Kiwanis Pathway is located in DeKalb and runs along the Kishwaukee River Between Lions Park and Hopkins Park. The setting is riverfront and open space.
Information	DeKalb Park District (815) 756-9939
County	DeKalb

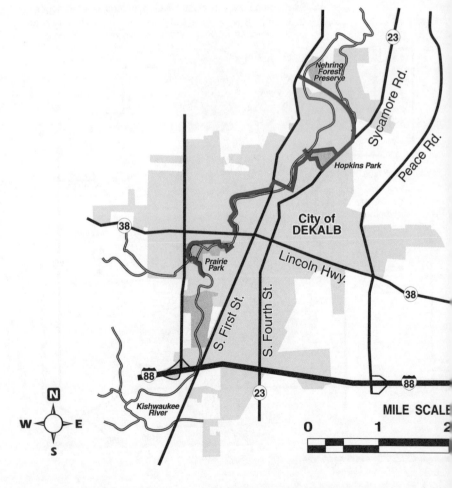

Kiwanis Trail

Trail Length	6.5 miles
Surface	Paved (10 feet), connecting low speed streets
Uses	Leisure bicycling, cross country skiing, in-line skating, hiking
Location & Setting	Located on the north side of the Rock River in Moline. It extends from 7th Street to 60th.
Information	Moline Park and Recreation Department (309) 797-0785
County	Rock Island

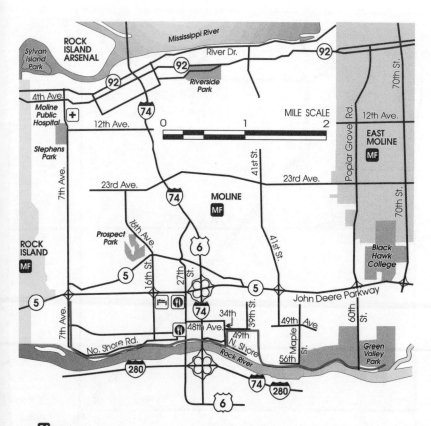

The trail is open from sunrise to sunset, year round. Food, lodging, sight-seeing facilities are readily available.

Lincoln Prairie Trail

Trail Length	16 miles
Surface	Asphalt
Uses	Leisure bicycling, hiking
Location & Setting	The trail connects the communities of Taylorville and Pana in central Illinois, and parallels Hwy 29. It is asphalt paved, 10-feet wide, and was built on old railroad grade. Setting is rural.
Information	Office of Community Development (217) 562-3109
County	Christian

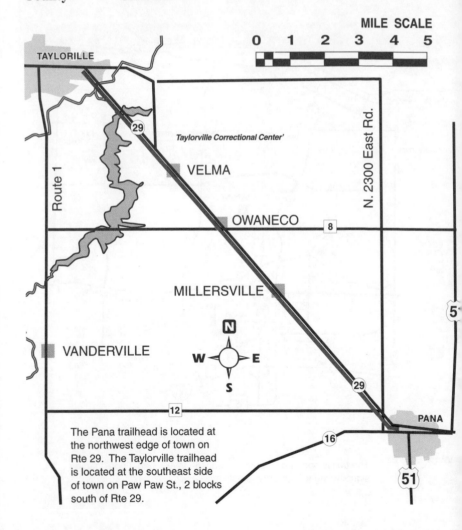

The Pana trailhead is located at the northwest edge of town on Rte 29. The Taylorville trailhead is located at the southeast side of town on Paw Paw St., 2 blocks south of Rte 29.

Lost Bridge Trail

Trail Length	5 miles
Surface	Paved
Uses	Leisure bicycling, in-line skating, hiking/jogging.
Location & Setting	The Lost Bridge Trail, stretching from Springfield's east side to the town of Rochester, is built on an old railroad right-of-way. There is a connecting trail to Rochester Community Park, with access to parking, water and restrooms. Dense trees line each side of the trail and shields bicyclists from nearby traffic noises.
Information	Village of Rochester (217) 498-7192
County	Sangamon

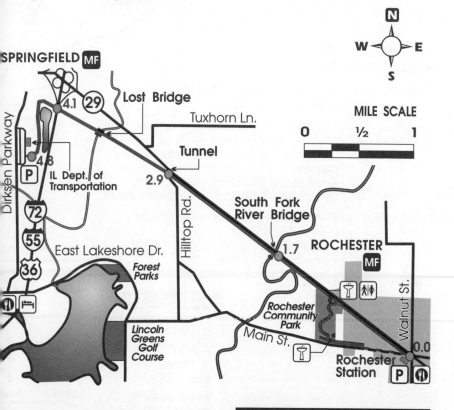

ROUTES

━━━━ Bicycling Trail
━━━━ Bikeway
━━━━ Roadway

FACILITIES

🛏 Lodging   P Parking
🚻 Restrooms   🅜 Refreshments
MF Multi Facilities   🚰 Water
   Available

Long Prairie Trail

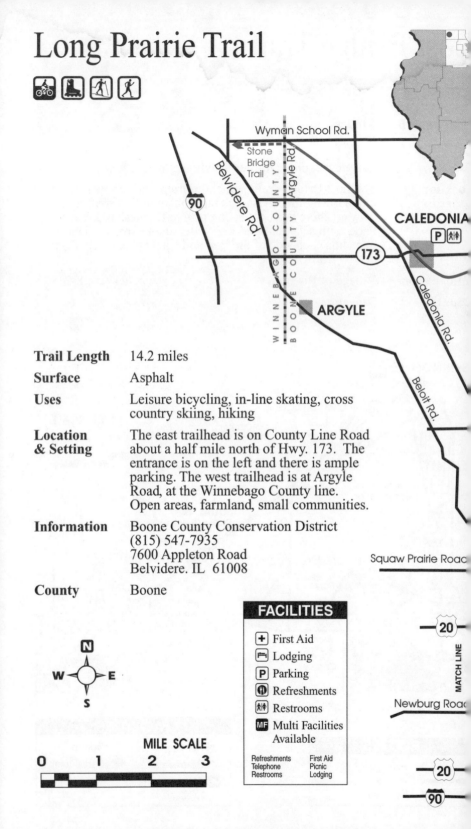

Trail Length	14.2 miles	
Surface	Asphalt	
Uses	Leisure bicycling, in-line skating, cross country skiing, hiking	
Location & Setting	The east trailhead is on County Line Road about a half mile north of Hwy. 173. The entrance is on the left and there is ample parking. The west trailhead is at Argyle Road, at the Winnebago County line. Open areas, farmland, small communities.	
Information	Boone County Conservation District (815) 547-7935 7600 Appleton Road Belvidere. IL 61008	
County	Boone	

FACILITIES

- ➕ First Aid
- 🏠 Lodging
- 🅿 Parking
- Ⓜ Refreshments
- 🚻 Restrooms
- **MF** Multi Facilities Available

Refreshments
Telephone
Restrooms

First Aid
Picnic
Lodging

MILE SCALE

0   1   2   3

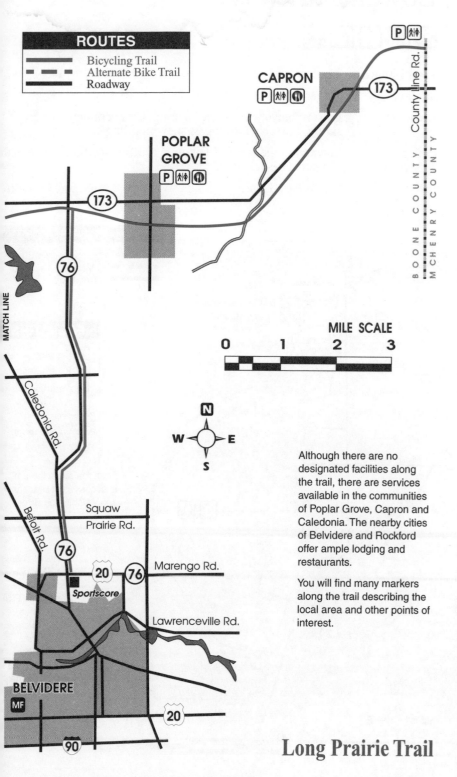

Although there are no
designated facilities along
the trail, there are services
available in the communities
of Poplar Grove, Capron and
Caledonia. The nearby cities
of Belvidere and Rockford
offer ample lodging and
restaurants.

You will find many markers
along the trail describing the
local area and other points of
interest.

Long Prairie Trail

Lowell Parkway

Trail Length	3 miles
Surface	Screenings
Uses	Leisure bicycling, hiking/jogging, cross-country skiing, horseback riding & snowmobiling
Location & Setting	Located in the town of Dixon in northwest Illinois. The path is a converted railbed.
Information	Dixon Park District (815) 284-3306
County	Lee

ROUTES

Bicycling Trail
Alternate Use Trail
Roadway

From the north the trail can be accessed at Lowell Park.

FACILITIES

P Parking
Restrooms
MF Multi Facilities Available

Refreshments   First Aid
Telephone   Picnic
Restrooms   Lodging

From the south the trail is accessed at Bradshaw and Washington Street.

Points of interest near Dixon include Castle Rock State Park, White Pines State Park, White Pines Forest State Park and John Deere's home.

MILE SCALE

0   1   2

Mattoon to Charleston Trail

Trail Length	12 miles
Surface	Limestone Screenings
Uses	Leisure bicycling, hiking
Location & Setting	The Mattoon to Charleston Trail is built along a ComEd right-of-way between the two cities. The surface is limestone screenings. The setting is open and farmland, and flat.
Information	Charleston Chamber of Commerce (217) 345-7041
County	Coles

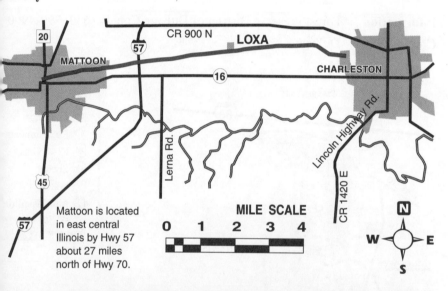

Mattoon is located in east central Illinois by Hwy 57 about 27 miles north of Hwy 70.

MILE SCALE
0 1 2 3 4

Right-of-Way Laws

Right-of-way means that one person has the right to go ahead of another. This applies to bicycle riders, vehicle drivers, and pedestrians. Right-of-way is something to give, not take. If others don't follow the rules, let them have the right-of -way.

At a four-way stop intersection, the driver or bicycle rider who arrives first at the intersection should be the first one to go. After making a complete stop, proceed only when it is safe to do so. Drivers and bicycle riders are expected to take their turns and go one by one through the intersection after they come to a complete stop.

At an unmarked intersection or crossing where there are no traffic signs or signals, the driver or bicycle rider on the left must yield to those on the right. When you drive out of an alley or driveway, you must stop and yield the right-of-way to pedestrians and vehicles before you cross the sidewalk or enter the street.

Emergency vehicles operating with their lights flashing and siren sounding always have the right-of-way. The law requires that you pull over to the side and stop it necessary.

McDowell Grove Forest Preserve

Trail Length	5.6 miles
Surface	Mowed turf
Uses	Fat tire bicycling, cross country skiing, hiking, horseback riding
Location & Setting	This preserve is located in southwest DuPage County on Raymond Road at McDowell Avenue between Ogden Avenue and the East-West Tollway (Hwy. 88) and south of Warrenville.
Information	Forest Preserve District of DuPage County (630) 790-4900
County	DuPage

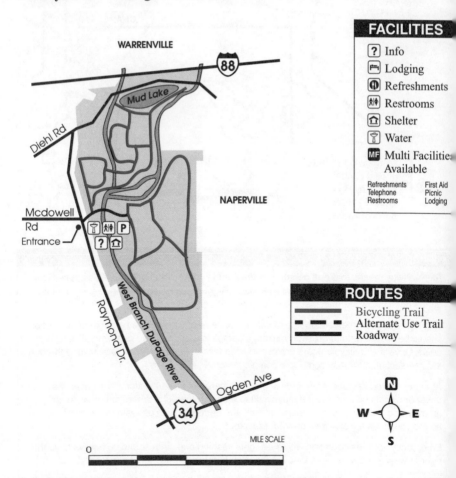

FACILITIES

- **?** Info
- **🛏** Lodging
- **🛈** Refreshments
- **🚻** Restrooms
- **🏠** Shelter
- **🚰** Water
- **MF** Multi Facilities Available

Refreshments	First Aid
Telephone	Picnic
Restrooms	Lodging

ROUTES

———	Bicycling Trail
– – –	Alternate Use Trail
———	Roadway

Moraine Hills State Park

Trail Length	8.9 miles
Surface	Limestone screenings
Uses	Leisure and fat tire bicycling, hiking
Location & Setting	Located 3 miles south of the city of McHenry, there is an easily recognized sign at the junction of Hwy. 176 and River Road directing you to parking. Wooded, wetlands, and is well groomed with many small hills and curves.
Information	Moraine Hills State Park (815) 385-1624
County	McHenry

Trails are one-way and color coded. *There are three loops:*
Lake Defiance- 3.72 miles with red markers
Leather Leaf Bog- 3.18 miles with blue markers
Fox River- 2.0 miles with
yellow markers

Moraine Hills State Park consists of 1,690 acres. There is trail access at McHenry Dam.

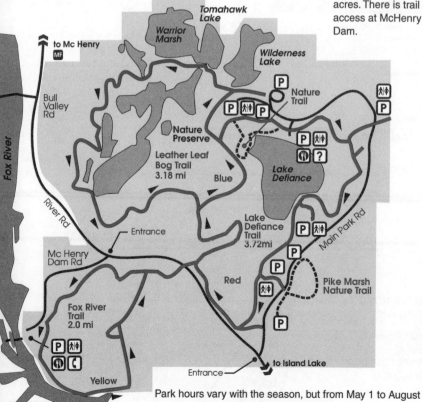

Park hours vary with the season, but from May 1 to August 31, the park is open from 6am to 9pm.

North Branch Bicycle Trail
Techny Trail

Trail Length	20 miles (plus bikeways)
Surface	Paved
Uses	Leisure bicycling, cross country skiing, hiking/jogging
Location & Setting	Open spaces, wooded—extends from the Chicago Botanic Gardens south approximately 20 miles to Caldwell and Devon Avenues in Chicago.
Information	Forest Preserve District of Cook County (708) 366-9420
County	Cook

POINTS OF INTEREST
- Ⓐ Chicago Botanic Garden
- Ⓑ Skokie Lagoons
- Ⓒ Blue Star Memorial Woods
- Ⓓ Glenview Woods
- Ⓔ Harms Woods
- Ⓕ Chick Evans Golf Course
- Ⓖ Linne Woods
- Ⓗ Miami Woods
- Ⓘ Clayton Smith Woods
- Ⓙ Whealan Pool
- Ⓚ Edgebrook Golf Course
- Ⓛ Billy Caldwell Golf Course

ROUTES
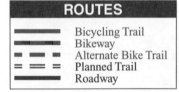

- ═══ Bicycling Trail
- ▬▬ Bikeway
- ▬ ▬ ▬ Alternate Bike Trail
- = = = Planned Trail
- ═══ Roadway

FACILITIES
- ? Info
- MF Multi Facilities Available

Refreshments — First Aid
Telephone — Picnic
Restrooms — Lodging

EMERGENCY ASSISTANCE

Forest Preserve Police at
708/366-8210 or
708/366-8211

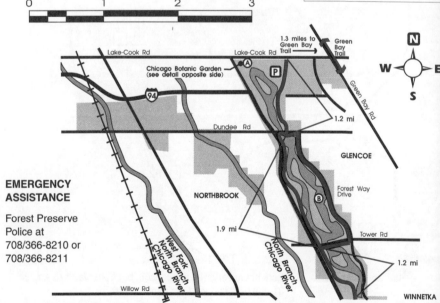

96

The trail winds along the North Branch of the Chicago River and the Skokie Lagoons, providing access to various picnic groves and communities in addition to the Botanic Gardens.

North Branch Bicycle Trail

North Shore Path

Trail Length	8.5 miles
Surface	Limestone screenings, paved
Uses	Leisure bicycling, cross country skiing, hiking/jogging
Location & Setting	Proceeds west from just south of Rock-land Rd. (Hwy. 176 in Lake Bluff to Hwy. 45 in Mundelein. Surburban, open and lightly wooded areas.
Information	Lake County Dept. of Transportation (847) 362-3950
County	Lake

FACILITIES

MF Multi Facilities
    Available

Refreshments   First Aid
Telephone   Picnic
Restrooms   Lodging

N
W — **E**
S

ROUTES

——— Bicycling Trail
– – – Alternate Bike Trail
——— Roadway

MILE SCALE

0   1   2   3   4

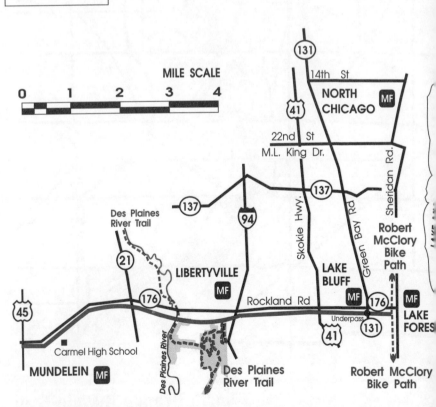

Oak Brook Bike Paths

Trail Length	17 miles (approximately) and some 5+ miles of designated bikeways
Surface	Paved, screenings
Uses	Leisure bicycling, in-line skating, hiking/jogging
Location & Setting	Oak Brook is located in east central DuPage County. The bike paths and bikeways are located throughout Oak Brook. There are multiple accesses to the paths as is parking. The setting is urban, open and wooded.
Information	Oak Brook Park District (630) 990-4233 1300 Forest Gate Road Oak Brook, IL 60521
County	DuPage

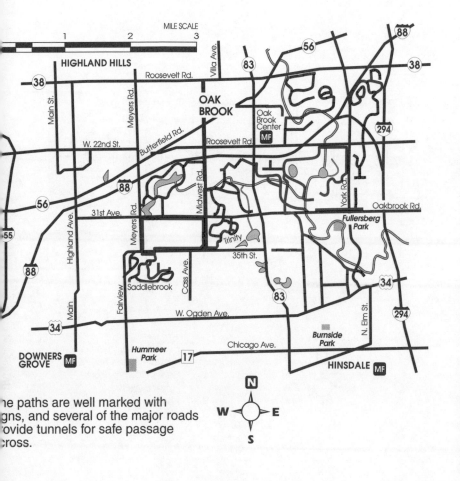

The paths are well marked with signs, and several of the major roads provide tunnels for safe passage across.

Old Plank Road Trail

Trail Length	26 miles
Surface	Crushed stone
Uses	Leisure bicycling, cross country skiing, hiking
Location & Setting	Located in Cook and Will Counties, the trail the trail will become a major link in the Grand Illinois Trail. It extends from Western Avenue in Park Forest to Cherry Hill Road east of Joliet. Plans include its extension to the I & M Canal State Trail. Hickory Creek Junction, a half mile north of the trail, serves as an access point with parking and a pedestrian bridge over Highway 30. The setting is urban with open and some wooded areas.
Information	Will County Forest Preserve (815) 727-8700
County	Cook, Will

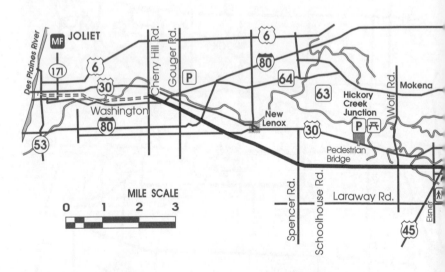

MILE SCALE

0   1   2   3

Restroom facilities are available at the Trolley Barn in the Frankfort Historic District, in addition to bicycle service and many shops.

FACILITIES

- 🔧 Bike Repair
- P Parking
- ⌷ Picnic
- 🚹🚺 Restrooms
- 🚰 Water
- **MF** Multi Facilities
  Available

Refreshments	First Aid
Telephone	Picnic
Restrooms	Lodging

ROUTES

━━━ Bicycling Trail
= = = Planned Trail
Roadway

RULES OF THE TRAIL

Hours of operation are from
dawn to dusk

No alcoholic beverages

No motorized vehicles

No camping or fires

Stay on the trail

Picking or damaging plants
on the trail is prohibited

Obey all posted signs

The METRA station, located between Park Forest and Matteson, provides transportation to the Chicago Loop. There is parking, bike racks and lockers at the Park Forest municipal parking lot.

From the eastern trailhead, the Sauk Trail Woods is located a half mile to the east. Plans are to acquire a railroad right-of-way in Chicago Heights to connect these trails.

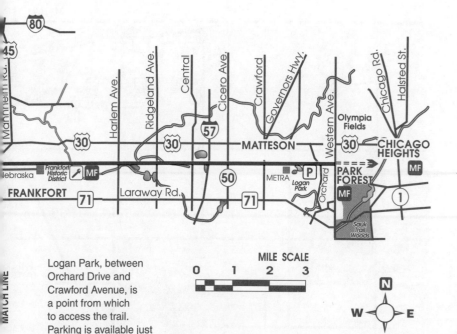

Logan Park, between Orchard Drive and Crawford Avenue, is a point from which to access the trail. Parking is available just south of the trail.

MILE SCALE

0   1   2   3

Old Plank Road Trail

Palos & Sag Valley Forest Preserve
I & M Canal TrailCook County

Trail Length	Palos is 30.0 miles, I & M Canal is 8.9 miles
Surface	Palos is Natural & groomed, I & M Canal is paved
Uses	Palos - Fat tire bicycling, hiking, horseback riding I & M Canal - Leisure bicycling, cross country skiing
Location & Setting	Palos located in southwest Cook County, mostly hilly and forested with many upland meadows, lakes ponds and sloughs. I & M Canal open and flat.
Information	Palos Forest Preserve (708) 361-1536
County	Cook

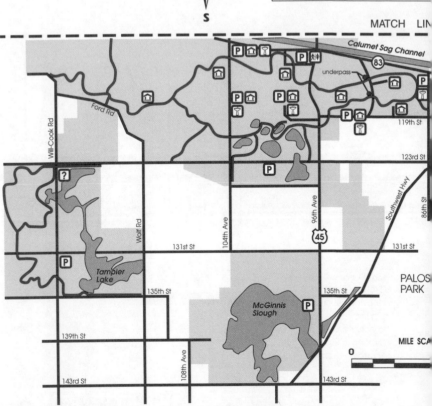

ROUTES
Bicycling Trail
Alternate Use Trail
Roadway

N
W E
S

MATCH LIN

Calumet Sag Channel

83

underpass

119th St

123rd St

Ford Rd

Will-Cook Rd

Wolf Rd

104th Ave

96th Ave

Southwest Hwy

86th

45

131st St

131st St

PALOS PARK

Tampier Lake

135th St

135th St

McGinnis Slough

139th St

108th Ave

143rd St

143rd St

MILE SCA

0

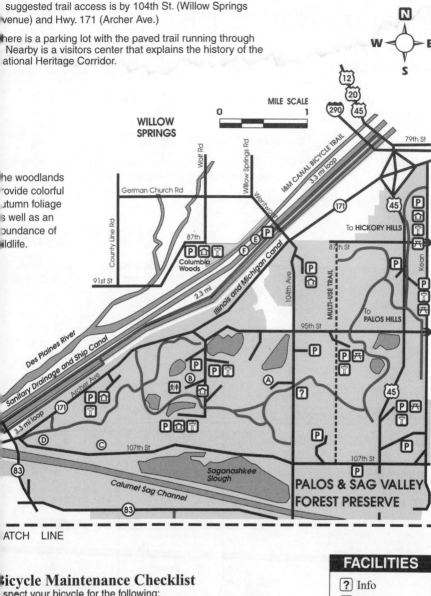

suggested trail access is by 104th St. (Willow Springs
venue) and Hwy. 171 (Archer Ave.)

here is a parking lot with the paved trail running through
Nearby is a visitors center that explains the history of the
ational Heritage Corridor.

he woodlands
rovide colorful
utumn foliage
s well as an
bundance of
ildlife.

WILLOW
SPRINGS

MILE SCALE

I&M CANAL BICYCLE TRAIL
3.3 mi loop

79th St

German Church Rd

Wolf Rd

Willow Springs Rd

Wentworth

County Line Rd

91st St

87th

Columbia
Woods

Illinois and Michigan Canal

2.3 mi

Des Plaines River

Sanitary Drainage and Ship Canal

Archer Ave

3.3 mi loop

171

171

To HICKORY HILLS

87th St

104th Ave

95th St

MULTI-USE TRAIL

To
PALOS HILLS

Keon

45

45

45

107th St

Saganashkee
Slough

Calumet Sag Channel

83

83

107th St

PALOS & SAG VALLEY
FOREST PRESERVE

ATCH LINE

Bicycle Maintenance Checklist
spect your bicycle for the following:

heels are securely attached, properly adjusted and spin freely
ith all spokes in place.

ll reflectors are clean and intact.

he seat and handlebars are adjusted to a comfortable position
ith all nuts and bolts tightened.

and grips are secure.

aliper brake pads are not worn and are properly adjusted.

FACILITIES

?	Info
P	Parking
🛆	Picnic
🏠	Shelter
🛆	Water
MF	Multi Facilities Available

Refreshments	First Aid
Telephone	Picnic
Restrooms	Lodging

Palos & Sag Valley Forest Preserve

Palatine Trail & Bikeway

Trail Length	15 miles (includes connecting bike routes)
Surface	Paved
Uses	Leisure bicycling, cross country skiing, hiking
Location & Setting	Palatine is located in northwest Cook County. Wooded area open spaces, connecting street bikeways, urban.
Information	Palatine Park District (847) 991-0333
County	Cook

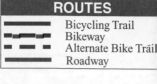

ROUTES
- Bicycling Trail
- Bikeway
- Alternate Bike Trail
- Roadway

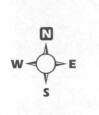

MILE SCALE (approx.)

0   1

Deer Grove
Bicycle Trail

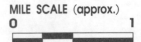

FACILITIES

MF Multi Facilities
Available

Refreshments	First Aid
Telephone	Picnic
Restrooms	Lodging

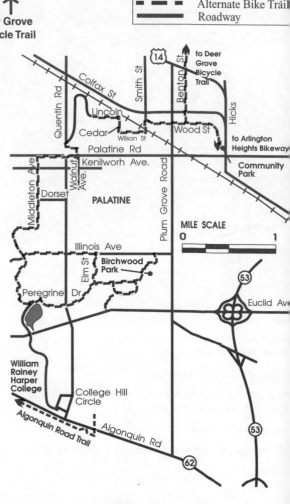

The Palatine Trail
extends throughout the
Palatine Park district.
Combining paved
trail with designated
side streets, Palatine
Trail provides access
to schools, Harper
College, neighborhood
parks, Palatine Hills
Golf Course, and other
points of interest.

Peace Road Trail

Trail Length	5 miles
Surface	Screenings
Uses	Leisure bicycling, cross country skiing, hiking
Location & Setting	The Peace Road Trail extends from Bethany Road in Sycamore to Pleasant Street in DeKalb. Current access to the Great Western Trail is by way of Airport Road. The setting is rural with farmland, woods and open areas.
Information	DeKalb County Forest Preserve Commission (815) 895-7191
County	DeKalb

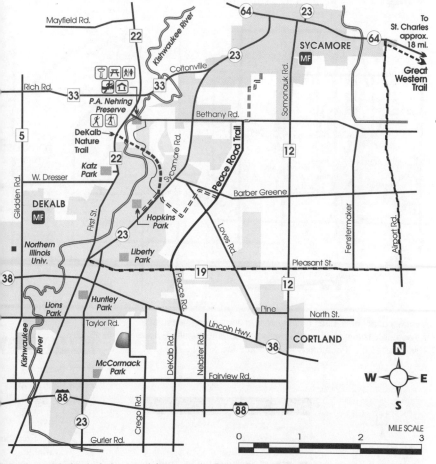

Planned construction includes a path between the Peace Road Trail and both Hopkins Park and the DeKalb Nature Trail. Also planned is an alternate route connecting to the Great Western Trail.

Pecatonica Prairie Path

Trail Length	21 miles
Surface	Ballast
Uses	Fat tire bicycling, hiking
Location & Setting	The trail follows an old railroad right-of-way through Stephenson and Winnebago counties. The eastern trailhead is off Meridian Road just south of Hwy. 20 and west of the city of Rockford. The western trailhead is south of the intersection of Hillcrest Road and River Road, off Hwy. 75 3 miles east of Freeport. The trails pass through open areas and farmland. Lightly wooded.
Information	Rockford Park District (815) 987-8800
County	Winnebago, Stephenson

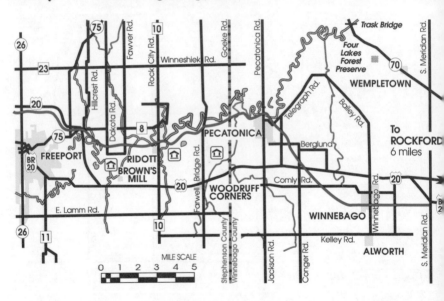

A variety of animals, birds and native wild flowers can be found along the corridor. The right-of-way is owned by Commonwealth Edison, which leases it to Pecatonica Prairie Path, Inc.

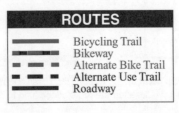

ROUTES

- ———— Bicycling Trail
- ———— Bikeway
- – – – Alternate Bike Trail
- ▬ ▬ ▬ Alternate Use Trail
- ———— Roadway

FACILITIES

- 🐾 Picnic
- 🚻 Restrooms
- ⌂ Shelter
- 🚰 Water
- **MF** Multi Facilities Available

Refreshments	First Aid
Telephone	Picnic
Restrooms	Lodging

Pimiteoui Trail

Trail Length	Approximately 5 miles
Surface	Paved
Uses	Leisure bicycling, hiking/jogging
Location & Setting	Located in the city of Peoria, south to north, from the Robert Mitchell Bridge to the Pioneer Parkway. Urban and open areas.
Information	Peoria Park District (309) 682-1200
County	Peoria

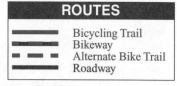

ROUTES

———	Bicycling Trail
———	Bikeway
– – –	Alternate Bike Trail
———	Roadway

ROUTE SLIP

Foot of Robert Michel Bridge along waterfront to Woodruff Park.

Cross Adams St., and then head east 75 feet to Abington St.

Follow Abington to Perry Ave., in front of Woodruff High School.

Turn north on Perry, through Springdale Cemetery and under Route 150 to Harvard Ave.

Continue on Harvard Ave., north to Lake Ave., then turn right on Prospect Rd.

Follow Prospect Rd. north for 9 blocks to Kingman Ave., and then turn left on Kingman Ave., following it west to Montclair Ave.

Turn right on Montclair and follow it north to Humbolt Ave., and then to Prospect by Junction City.

Continue along the eastern edge of the railway to Pioneer Parkway.

MILE SCALE

Potawatomi Trail

Trail Length	7 miles
Surface	Natural – groomed
Uses	Mountain bicycling, hiking, horseback riding
Location & Setting	The Powawatomi Trail is located in Pekin at McNaughton Park. The trail begins and ends at the Totem Pole, behind the stables, and is also open to hiking and horseback riding. Red markers indicate the main trail. The park covers some 700-acres of beautiful woodland and meadows.
Information	Pekin Park District Recreation Department (309) 347-7275
County	Tazewell

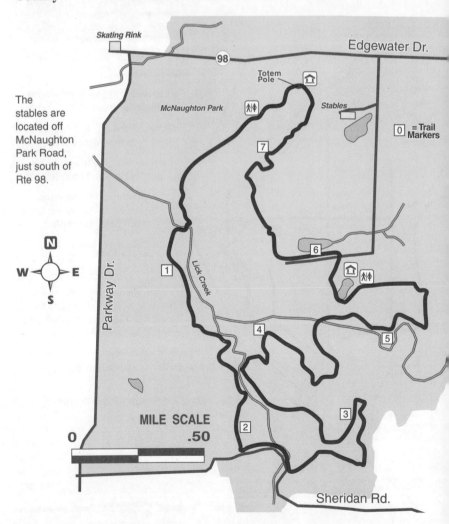

The stables are located off McNaughton Park Road, just south of Rte 98.

Prairie Trail

Trail Length	18 miles
Surface	Limestone screenings (some ballast)
Uses	Leisure bicycling, fat tire bicycling, cross country skiing, hiking, horseback riding, snowmobiling
Location & Setting	From Crystal Lake north to the Wisconsin State Line. Open space, wooded areas, small communities.
Information	McHenry County Conservation District (815) 678-4431
County	McHenry

ROUTES

━━━ Bicycling Trail
- - - Alternate Bike Trail
━━━ Roadway

Richmond is an interesting small community with several antique shops. The trail crosses Hwy. 173 just west of Hwy. 31. There is no designated parking.

FACILITIES

P Parking
Ⓜ Refreshments
🚻 Restrooms
MF Multi Facilities Available

Refreshments   First Aid
Telephone   Picnic
Restrooms   Lodging

Fat tires are recommended as the trail is somewhat rough from equestrian use.

Pratts Wayne Woods Forest Preserve

Trail Length	7.3 miles
Surface	Mowed turf
Uses	Fat tire bicycling, cross country skiing, hiking, horseback riding
Location & Setting	Located in the northwest corner of DuPage County between Wayne and Barlett. Access from Powis Road a mile north of Army Trail Road or from the Illinois Prairie Path. It's 2,600 acres include savannas, marshes, meadows and prairies. Wildlife and plants abound.
Information	Forest Preserve District of DuPage County (630) 790-4900
County	DuPage

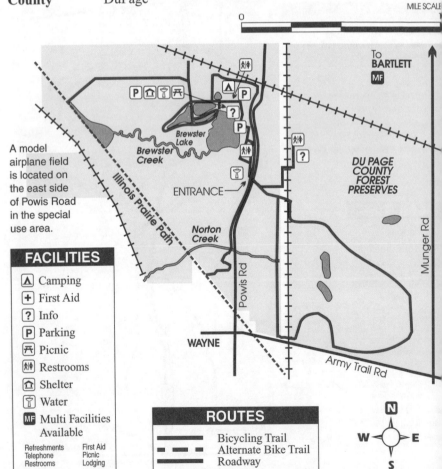

A model airplane field is located on the east side of Powis Road in the special use area.

FACILITIES

- ◬ Camping
- ✚ First Aid
- ? Info
- P Parking
- 🎋 Picnic
- 🚻 Restrooms
- ⌂ Shelter
- 🚰 Water
- MF Multi Facilities Available

Refreshments   First Aid
Telephone   Picnic
Restrooms   Lodging

ROUTES

— Bicycling Trail
- - - Alternate Bike Trail
— Roadway

Pyramid State Park

Trail Length	16.5 miles
Surface	Natural – groomed
Uses	Mountain bicycling, hiking, horseback riding
Location & Setting	Pyramid State Park, with 2,528-acres, consists of heavily forested hills with many lakes and ponds. It is located about 5 miles south of Pinckneyville, off Routes 127/13 in southern Illinois. The surface is dirt and generally flat with some hills. Tent and trail camping is available, with both Class C & D campsites. Canoeing is popular.
Information	Pyramid State Park (618) 357-2574
County	Perry

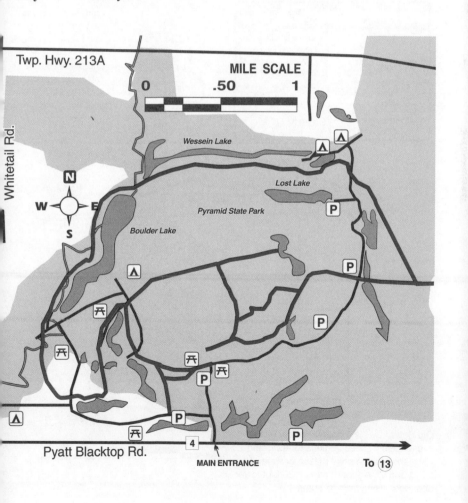

Red Hills State Park

Trail Length	6 miles
Surface	Screenings, natural
Uses	Leisure and fat tire bicycling (moderate) and hiking
Location & Setting	Located in southeastern Illinois between Olney and Lawrenceville on U.S. Route 50. The park consists of 948 acres with wooded hills, deep ravines, meadows and year round springs.
Information	Red Hills State Park (618) 936-2469
County	Lawrence

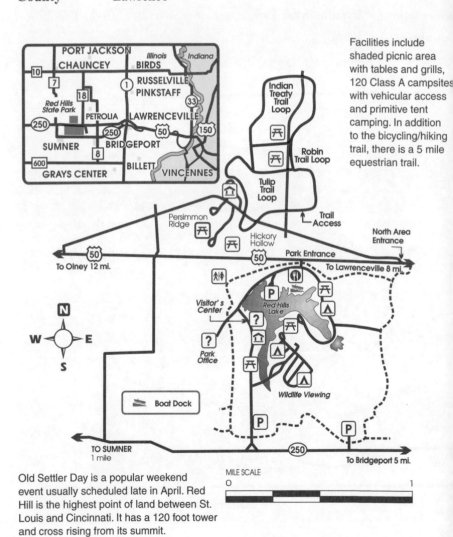

Facilities include shaded picnic area with tables and grills, 120 Class A campsites with vehicular access and primitive tent camping. In addition to the bicycling/hiking trail, there is a 5 mile equestrian trail.

Old Settler Day is a popular weekend event usually scheduled late in April. Red Hill is the highest point of land between St. Louis and Cincinnati. It has a 120 foot tower and cross rising from its summit.

MILE SCALE
0   1

River Trail of Illinois

Trail Length	10.8 miles
Surface	Paved, limestone screenings
Uses	Leisure bicycling, hiking
Location & Setting	Located between Morton and East Peoria. Urban, open and wooded areas, small hills.
Information	Fond Du Lac Park District (309) 699-3923
County	Tazewell

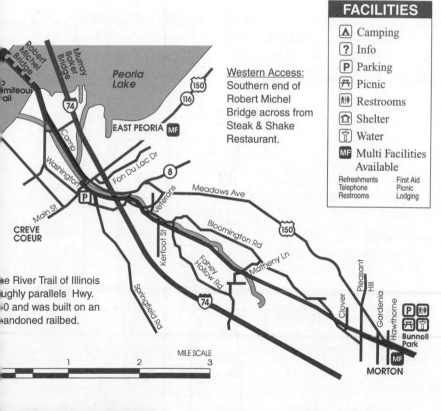

Western Access: Southern end of Robert Michel Bridge across from Steak & Shake Restaurant.

FACILITIES

- ▲ Camping
- ? Info
- P Parking
- 🛆 Picnic
- 👫 Restrooms
- 🏠 Shelter
- 🍵 Water
- **MF** Multi Facilities Available

Refreshments   First Aid
Telephone   Picnic
Restrooms   Lodging

The River Trail of Illinois roughly parallels Hwy. 150 and was built on an abandoned railbed.

ROUTES

Bicycling Trail
Alternate Bike Trail
Alternate Use Trail
Roadway

Eastern Access: Across from K-Mart and Golden Corral Restaurant.

Robert McClory Bike Path

Trail Length	25 miles
Surface	Limestone screenings, paved
Uses	Leisure bicycling, cross country skiing, hiking/jogging
Location & Setting	The trail runs north and south from the Cook County line (lake Cook Road) to the Wisconsin border. The setting is surburban, open and lightly wooded areas.
Information	Lake County Dept. of Transportation (847) 362-5950
County	Lake

Some of the surface is limestone screenings. The remainder is paved, or street/sidewalk connections.

Screenings:

Highland Park
 - Ravinia Park to Laurel (2 mi.)

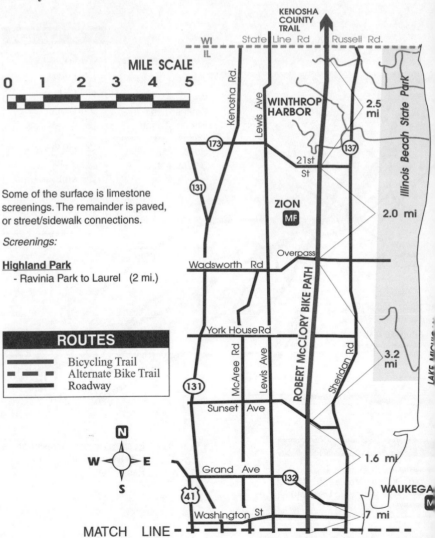

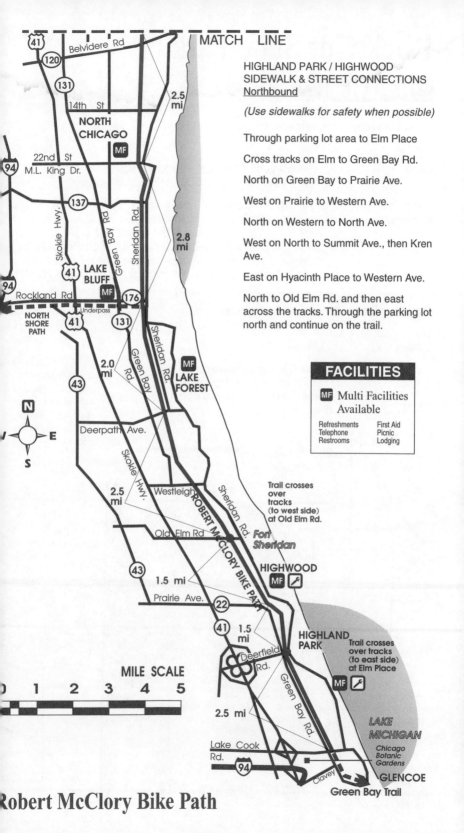

MATCH LINE

**HIGHLAND PARK / HIGHWOOD
SIDEWALK & STREET CONNECTIONS
Northbound**

(Use sidewalks for safety when possible)

Through parking lot area to Elm Place

Cross tracks on Elm to Green Bay Rd.

North on Green Bay to Prairie Ave.

West on Prairie to Western Ave.

North on Western to North Ave.

West on North to Summit Ave., then Kren Ave.

East on Hyacinth Place to Western Ave.

North to Old Elm Rd. and then east across the tracks. Through the parking lot north and continue on the trail.

FACILITIES

MF Multi Facilities Available

Refreshments	First Aid
Telephone	Picnic
Restrooms	Lodging

Belvidere Rd.

14th St

NORTH CHICAGO

22nd St
M.L. King Dr.

Skokie Hwy.

Green Bay Rd.

Sheridan Rd.

LAKE BLUFF

Rockland Rd.

NORTH SHORE PATH

Underpass

2.5 mi

2.8 mi

2.0 mi

Green Bay Rd.

Sheridan Rd.

MF LAKE FOREST

Deerpath Ave.

Skokie Hwy.

2.5 mi

Westleigh

Old Elm Rd.

ROBERT McCLORY BIKE PATH

Sheridan Rd.

Trail crosses over tracks (to west side) at Old Elm Rd.

Fort Sheridan

HIGHWOOD
MF

1.5 mi

Prairie Ave.

1.5 mi

Deerfield Rd.

HIGHLAND PARK

Trail crosses over tracks (to east side) at Elm Place

MF

Green Bay Rd.

MILE SCALE

0 1 2 3 4 5

2.5 mi

Lake Cook Rd.

LAKE MICHIGAN

Chicago Botanic Gardens

Clavey

GLENCOE

Green Bay Trail

Robert McClory Bike Path

Rock Cut State Park

Trail Length	10 miles
Surface	Dirt
Uses	Fat tire bicycling (easy to moderate), cross country skiing, hiking, horseback riding, snowmobiling
Location & Setting	Located in Winnebago County northeast of Rockford, and approximately 80 miles northwest of Chicago. From I-90, exit at East Riverside Blvd. and head west for 1 mile, then turn right on McFarland Road to Harlem Road (dead end). Turn east (right) for a little over a mile, over I-90, to the Park entrance. Terrain is rugged, rocky with woods and small hills.
Information	Rock Cut State Park (815) 885-3311
	Emergency 911
County	Winnebago

There are individual routes for hiking, bicycling, horseback riding and snowmobiling. The track varies from 5 to 10 feet wide.

Rock Cut State Park consists of 3,096 acres. Facilities include concessions, restrooms, water, boat rental and canoe access.

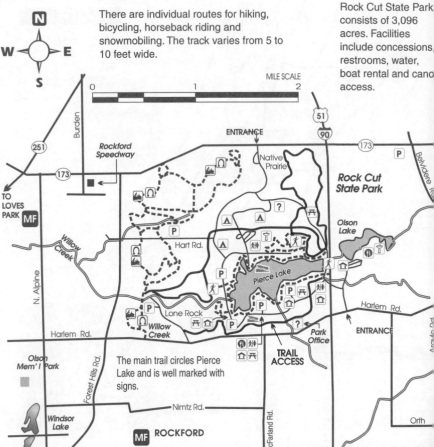

The main trail circles Pierce Lake and is well marked with signs.

Rock River & Sportscore Recreation Path

Trail Length	8 miles
Surface	Asphalt
Uses	Leisure bicycling, in-line skating, cross country skiing, hiking/jogging
Location & Setting	The path follows the Rock River in Rockford from Walnut Street north through Veterans Memorial Park/Sportscore to Harlem Road. The setting is urban.
Information	Rockford Park District (815) 987-8800
County	Winnebago

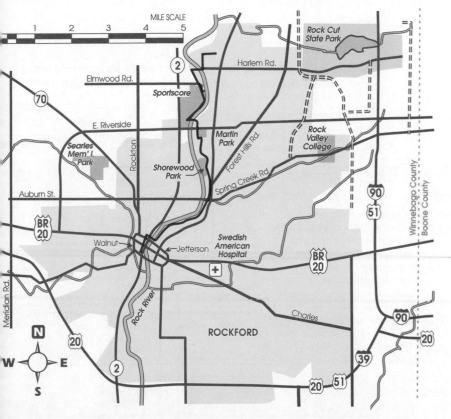

The Sportscore joins the Rock River Path at Elmwood Road, proceeds along Brown Beach Road jogging west, then northeast along Harlem Road and across the Rock River. The path crosses the Rock River at Jefferson Street, Riverside Blvd. and Harlem Road. There are numerous points of interest along the path.

Rock Island State Trail

Trail Length	28.3 miles
Surface	Limestone screenings
Uses	Leisure bicycling, cross country skiing, hiking
Location & Setting	Stretches from Pioneer Parkway along an old railroad right-of-way through the communities of Dunlap, Princeville, and Wyoming to the edge of Toulon in Stark County northwest of Peoria. The Trail lies in a vast plain formerly occupied by tallgrass prairie. The land is dominated by cultivated fields but numerous patches of prairie and stands of trees are scattered along the route.
Information	Friends of the Rock Island Trail (309) 694-3196 Rock Island Trail State Park (309) 695-2228
County	Peoria, Stark

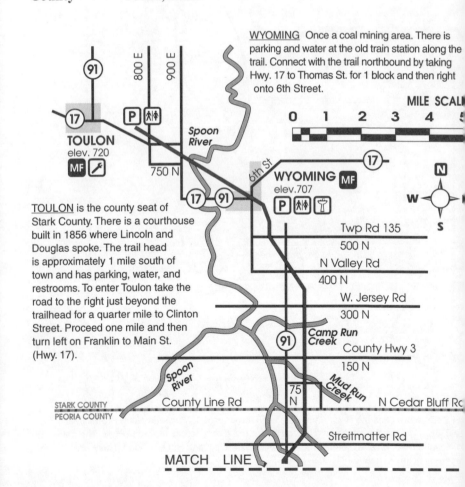

WYOMING Once a coal mining area. There is parking and water at the old train station along the trail. Connect with the trail northbound by taking Hwy. 17 to Thomas St. for 1 block and then right onto 6th Street.

TOULON is the county seat of Stark County. There is a courthouse built in 1856 where Lincoln and Douglas spoke. The trail head is approximately 1 mile south of town and has parking, water, and restrooms. To enter Toulon take the road to the right just beyond the trailhead for a quarter mile to Clinton Street. Proceed one mile and then turn left on Franklin to Main St. (Hwy. 17).

MATCH LINE

OTHER FEATURES OF THE ROCK ISLAND TRAIL INCLUDE:

An arched culvert with wing wall construction of massive limestone blocks, located about 2 miles north of Alta. A steel trestle bridge, circa 1910, spanning the Spoon River. A rehabilitated rail station in Wyoming, which was built in 1871.

ROUTES

━━━	Bicycling Trail
━━━	Roadway

PRINCEVILLE You cross the Santa Fe railroad tracks as you enter the town from the south. Just beyond the tracks is a park with restrooms and a picnic area. The trail connects through city streets- proceed on Walnut to North Ave. a short distance and left onto North Town Rd. for a half mile. Turn left on a marked single lane road to connect with the trail again.

FACILITIES

🔧	Bike Repair
?	Info
P	Parking
🛆	Picnic
🚻	Restrooms
🚰	Water
MF	Multi Facilities Available

Refreshments	First Aid
Telephone	Picnic
Restrooms	Lodging

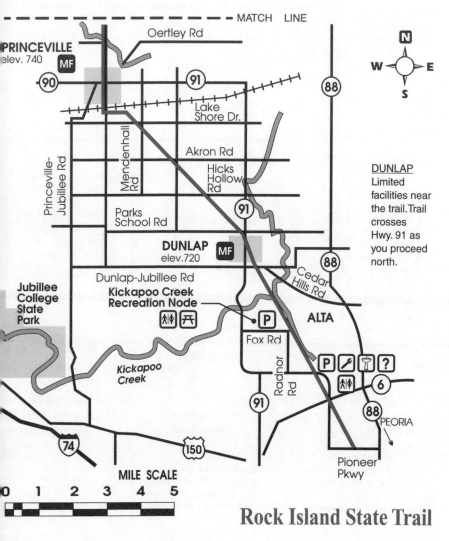

DUNLAP
Limited facilities near the trail. Trail crosses Hwy. 91 as you proceed north.

Rock Island State Trail

Salt Creek Bicycle Trail

Trail Length	6.6 miles
Surface	Paved
Uses	Leisure bicycling, cross country skiing, jogging
Location & Setting	Located in west central Cook County. Bordered clockwise by the communities of Oakbrook, Westchester, Brookfield, LaGrange Park, LaGrange and Hinsdale. The Salt Creek Trail starts in Bemis Woods South and continues east to Brookfield Woods, directly across from the Brookfield Zoo. As the trail follows Salt Creek, it provides access to various picnic groves and other points of interest. The trail may be accessed from Ogden Avenue, just east of Wolf Road, or from 31st Street between First Avenue and Prairie Avenue.
Information	Forest Preserve District of Cook County (708) 366-9420 Emergency Assistance (708) 366-8210
County	Cook

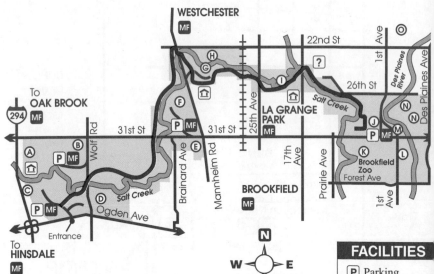

POINTS OF INTEREST

A. Meadow Lark Golf Course
B. Bemis Woods North
C. Bemis Woods South
D. Salt Creek Nursery
E. La Grange Park Woods
F. Possum Hollow Woods
G. Brezina Woods
H. Westchester Woods

I. 26th Street Woods
J. Brookfield Woods
K. Brookfield Zoo
L. Zoo Woods
M. McCormick Woods
N. National Grove-North & South
O. Miller Meadows

FACILITIES

P Parking
Shelter
MF Multi Facilities Available

Refreshments   First Aid
Telephone   Picnic
Restrooms   Lodging

Stone Bridge Trail

Trail Length	5.75 miles
Surface	Screenings
Uses	Leisure bicycling, cross country skiing, jogging, snowmobiling
Location & Setting	The trail is built on an abandoned railbed and begins at McCurry Road in Roscoe then proceeds southeast to the Boone county line. The setting is rural with wide open areas and farmland.
Information	Rockford Park District	(815) 987-8865
County	Winnebago

The Stone Bridge Trail joins the Long Prairie Trail at the Boone County line.

ROUTES

——————— Bicycling Trail
= = = Planned Trail
——————— Roadway

FACILITIES

P Parking

MF Multi Facilities Available

Refreshments   First Aid
Telephone   Picnic
Restrooms   Lodging

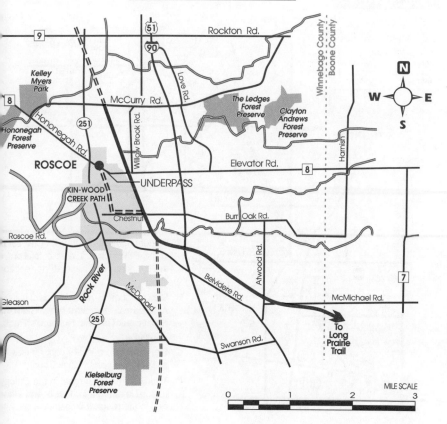

Thorn Creek Forest Preserve

Trail Length	8.0 miles
Surface	Paved
Uses	Leisure bicycling, cross country skiing, jogging
Location & Setting	The Thorn Creek Bicycle Trail is located in far south Cook County. One section consists of trail through the Sauk Trail lake area and another winds through Lansing Woods and North Creek Meadow. A future extension will link these sections. Access the western section along Ashland Avenue, and the eastern section from either Glenwood-Lansing Road or 183rd Street east of Torrence Avenue. It is bounded clockwise by the communities of South Holland, Lansing, Chicago Heights, South Chicago Heights, Park Forest, Olympia Fields, Glenwood and Thornton.
Information	Forest Preserve District of Cook County (708) 366-8210
County	Cook

FACILITIES

- **P** Parking
- **MF** Multi Facilities Available

Refreshments	First Aid
Telephone	Picnic
Restrooms	Lodging

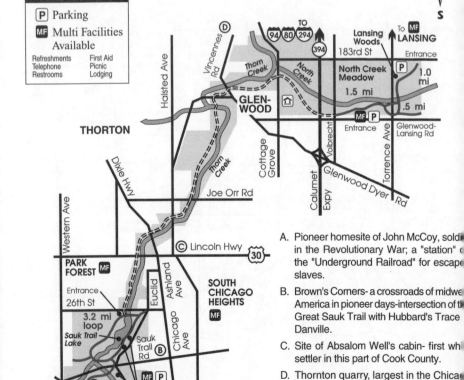

A. Pioneer homesite of John McCoy, soldi in the Revolutionary War; a "station" the "Underground Railroad" for escape slaves.

B. Brown's Corners- a crossroads of midwe America in pioneer days-intersection of t Great Sauk Trail with Hubbard's Trace Danville.

C. Site of Absalom Well's cabin- first wh settler in this part of Cook County.

D. Thornton quarry, largest in the Chica region, is notable for fossils and a co reef in the Niagara limestone.

Tinley Creek Forest Preserve

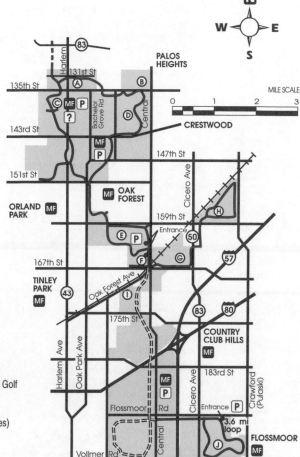

Trail Length	23.5 miles
Surface	Paved
Uses	Leisure bicycling, cross country skiing, jogging
Location & Setting	The Tinley Creek Bicycle Trail is located in southwestern Cook County. The trail passes through gently rolling country, forests, prairies and alongside wetlands. It is bordered (clockwise) by the communities of Palos Heights, Crestwood, Oak Forest, Country Club Hills, Flossmoor, Tinley Park and Orland Park.
Information	Forest Preserve District of Cook County (708) 366-9420
	Forest Pres. Police Emergency Assistance (708) 366-8210
County	Cook

...ause along 159th Street, ...st east of Oak Park ...venue, for an unusual ...ew of the Chicago ...kyline, approximately 20 ...iles to the northeast. ...here are accesses and ...arking along Central ...venue between 159th ...treet and 175th Street ...the northern section. ...ccess and parking to ...e southern loop is ...vailable off both Vollmer ...nd Flossmoor Roads. A ...ture extension will link ...ese two sections.

A. Arrowhead Lake Access Area
B. Elizabeth A. Conkey Forest
C. Turtlehead Lake Access Area
D. Rubio Woods
E. The George W. Dunne National Golf Course
F. Yankee Woods
G. Midlothian Reservoir (Twin Lakes)
H. Midlothian Meadows
I. St. Mihiel West
J. Vollmer Road Picnic

Tunnel Hill State Trail

Trail Length	44.5 miles* *(includes 2.3 mile Harrisburg ext.)*
Surface	Crushed stone
Uses	Leisure biking, hiking
Location & Setting	The Tunnel Hill Trail, when completed, will extend over 44 miles connecting the towns of Harrisburg to the north with Karnak to the south. It is being built on old railbed. Facilities are available at most of the 8 communities along its route. The trail parallels the west side of Hwy 45 south to Bloomfield, where it crosses to the east, then west again 3 miles south of Vienna paralleling Hwy 3 to Karnak.
Information	Tunnel Hill State Trail (618)658-2168
	Shawnee National Forest Forest Supervisor (800) MY WOODS (699-6637)
County	Saline, Williamson and Johnson

* Tunnel Hill to Vienna & Harrisburg ext. = 17.5 miles *complete*

Tunnel Hill to Harrsiburg = 17 mile

Vienna to Karnak = 10 miles *planned*

NEW BURNSIDE

4 miles

TUNNEL HILL

45

4

17.5 miles

Shawnee National Forest

MATCH LINE

24

45

147

VIENNA

146

146

24

10 miles

Little Black Slough Preserve

Heron Pond Preserve

45

N
W E
S

BELKNAP

169

KARNAK

3

0 1 2 3 4

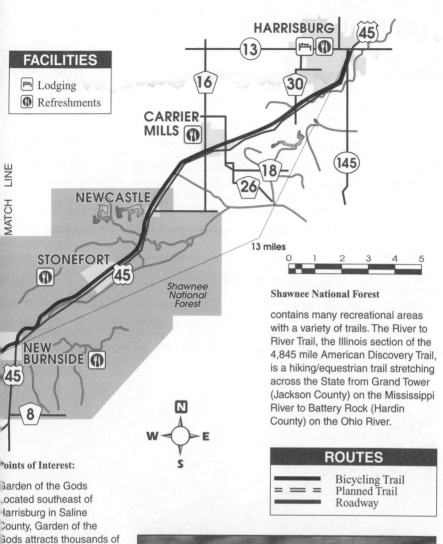

FACILITIES

🛏 Lodging
🍴 Refreshments

MATCH LINE

HARRISBURG 🛏🍴 (45)

(13)

(16)

(30)

CARRIER MILLS 🍴

(18)

(26)

(145)

NEWCASTLE 🎵

STONEFORT 🍴 (45)

Shawnee National Forest

NEW BURNSIDE 🍴

(45)

(8)

N
W ⬥ E
S

13 miles

0 1 2 3 4 5

Shawnee National Forest

contains many recreational areas with a variety of trails. The River to River Trail, the Illinois section of the 4,845 mile American Discovery Trail, is a hiking/equestrian trail stretching across the State from Grand Tower (Jackson County) on the Mississippi River to Battery Rock (Hardin County) on the Ohio River.

ROUTES

— Bicycling Trail
= = = Planned Trail
— Roadway

Points of Interest:

Garden of the Gods Located southeast of Harrisburg in Saline County, Garden of the Gods attracts thousands of visitors each year with its incredible rock formations, such as Camel Rock, Devil's Needle, Noah's Ark, Anvil Rock, and Tower of Babel. Eight miles of hiking trails bring visitors to the rock formations. The rocks can be climbed as well as viewed. The best time of year is the fall when the Shawnee Hills form a fiery backdrop to the formations. For more information call 618/287-2001.

Tunnel Hill Trail

Vadalabene Bike Trail

Trail Length	19 miles
Surface	Paved
Uses	Leisure bicycling, hiking
Location & Setting	This path follows Route 100 between Alton, through Grafton and to Pere Marquette State Park. The bikeway is bordered by towering limestone cliffs and the Mississippi River, and is a recreational destination for bicycle enthusiasts.
	Illinois Dept. of Transportation (618) 346-3100
Information	Southern Illinois Tourism Council Box 286 Belleville, IL 62222
County	Madison, Jersey

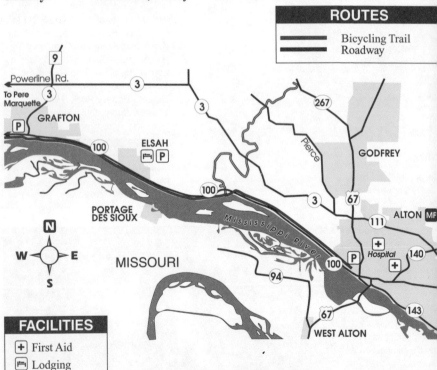

The northern section follows the wide paved shoulders of the McAdams Parkway to Grafton. The southern section is a separate paved path built on an abandoned railroad line at the base of the bluffs. There are parking areas along and at each end of the bikeway. Pause to visit the historic town of Grafton and Elsah with their antique shops.

Vadalabene Nature Trail

Trail Length	7.4 miles
Surface	Asphalt (12 feet wide)
Uses	Leisure bicycling, hiking, in-line skating
Location & Setting	Located between Esic Drive in Edwardsville and Lake Drive, east of Granite City. It goes through the Southern Illinois University campus. Setting is rural, with farmland, open areas, woods. The communities at either trailhead have full service facilities.
Information	Madison County Transit Authority (800) 628-7433
County	Madison

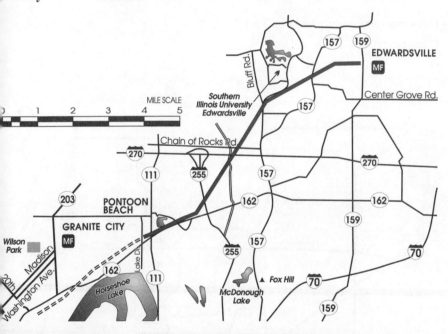

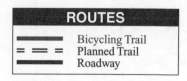

FACILITIES

- ✚ First Aid
- 🏠 Lodging
- P Parking
- **MF** Multi Facilities Available

Refreshments	First Aid
Telephone	Picnic
Restrooms	Lodging

When completed, the trail will extend from the Market Basket in Edwardsville to Washington Avenue in Granite City. This trail is isolated. It should be used only in groups and in daylight.

ROUTES

────────	Bicycling Trail
= = =	Planned Trail
────────	Roadway

Vernon Hills Trails

	Century Park	Deerpath
Trail Length	2.9 miles (loops)	1.25 miles
Surface	Paved	
Uses	Leisure bicycling, in-line skating, cross country skiing, hiking/jogging	
Location & Setting	Vernon Hills is located in central Lake County.	

	Century Park	**Deerpath**
	Route 60 west of Route 21 to Lakeview Parkway. Turn north for ½ mile to the park.	Route 21 (Milwaukee Avenue) past Lakeview Parkway to Deerpath Drive. Turn south and proceed to Cherokee Road. Turn east (left) to Deerpath Park.

Information	Vernon Hills Park District	(847) 367-7270
County	Lake	

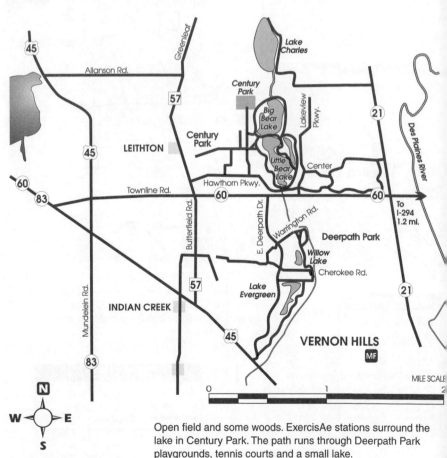

Open field and some woods. ExercisAe stations surround the lake in Century Park. The path runs through Deerpath Park playgrounds, tennis courts and a small lake.

Veteran Acres Park

Trail Length	Approximately 7.5 miles
Surface	Natural
Uses	Fat tire bicycling, cross country skiing, hiking
Location Setting	Located on the north side of Crystal Lake. Access from Terra Cotta Road from the south or Walkup Road from the west.
Information	Crystal Lake Park District (815) 459-0680
County	McHenry

Sterne's Woods can be accessed from Veteran Acres
and has about two miles of dirt road open to hiking.

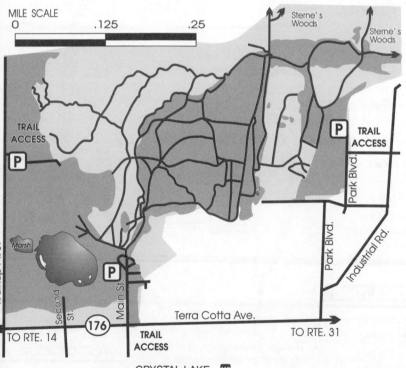

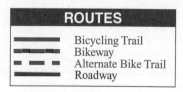

Virgil L. Gilman Nature Trail

Trail Length	10.5 miles	
Surface	Paved	
Uses	Leisure bicycling, cross country skiing, hiking	
Location & Setting	The trail stretches west uninterrupted past farmlands straddling the Kane and Kendall County border. The Virgil Gilman Trail passes rural, urban and suburban areas.	
Information	Fox River Park District	(630) 897-0516
County	Kane	

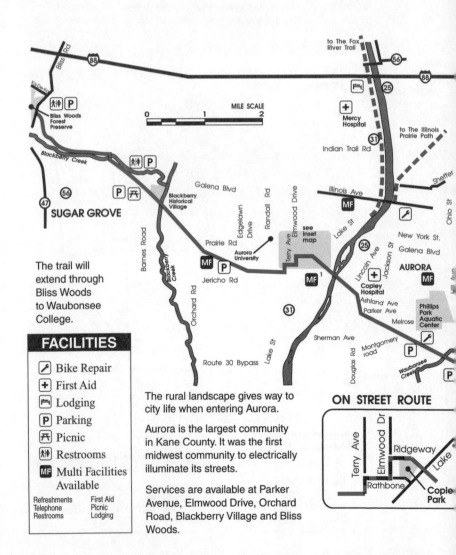

The trail will extend through Bliss Woods to Waubonsee College.

FACILITIES

- 🔧 Bike Repair
- ➕ First Aid
- 🛏 Lodging
- 🅿 Parking
- 🍽 Picnic
- 🚻 Restrooms
- **MF** Multi Facilities Available

Refreshments	First Aid
Telephone	Picnic
Restrooms	Lodging

The rural landscape gives way to city life when entering Aurora.

Aurora is the largest community in Kane County. It was the first midwest community to electrically illuminate its streets.

Services are available at Parker Avenue, Elmwood Drive, Orchard Road, Blackberry Village and Bliss Woods.

ON STREET ROUTE

130

Waterfall Glen Forest Preserve

Trail Length	8.5 miles (developed)
Surface	Limestone screenings
Uses	Leisure and fat tire bicycling,cross country skiing, hiking
Location Setting	Southeast corner of DuPage County, the trail circles Argonne National Laboratory. Forests, prairie, open areas.
Information	Forest Preserve District of DuPage County (630) 933-7248
County	DuPage

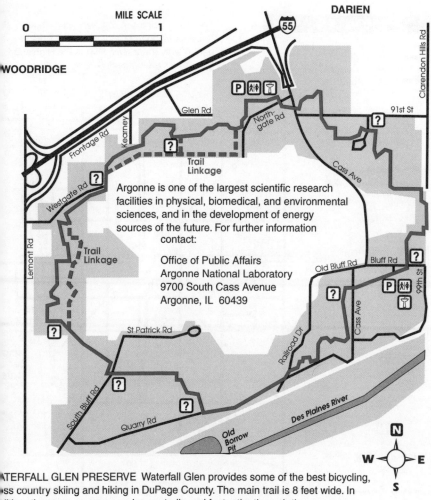

WATERFALL GLEN PRESERVE Waterfall Glen provides some of the best bicycling, cross country skiing and hiking in DuPage County. The main trail is 8 feet wide. In addition, there are many mowed grass trails and footpaths through the preserve.

Zion Bicycle Path

Trail Length	6.5 miles
Surface	Paved
Uses	Leisure bicycling, in-line skating, jogging
Location & Setting	This bicycle path and bikeway is located in the community of Zion in far northeastern Illinois. The setting is surburban.
Information	Zion Park District (847) 746-5500
County	Lake

There is a trail extension planned that will run west along the Commonwealth Edison right-of-way (near Hwy. 173) to the Highland Meadows development.

ROUTES

Bicycling Trail
Bikeway
Alternate Bike Trail
Roadway

FACILITIES

- **?** Info
- **P** Parking
- **🎑** Picnic
- **🍴** Refreshments
- **🚻** Restrooms
- **🚰** Water
- **MF** Multi Facilities Available

Refreshments   First Aid
Telephone   Picnic
Restrooms   Lodging

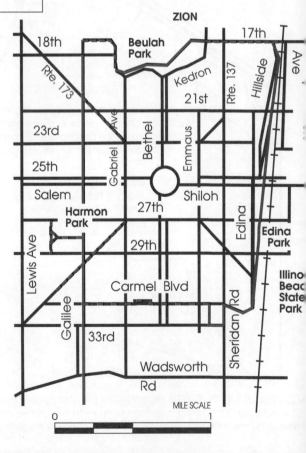

Additional Trails

BARTLETT'S TRAILS & BIKEWAYS

Trail Length	15 miles
Location & Setting	Bartlett. There is a trailhead on Route 50 between Routes 59 and 43 and at the intersection of Routes 59 and 6.
Information	Bartlett Park District (630) 837-6568
County	Cook

BELLEVILLE'S TRAILS & BIKEWAYS

Trail Length	6 miles
Surface	Crushed stone
Location & Setting	East Belleville. Trailheads at the junction of Routes 44 and 89 and the junction of Routes 158 and 159.
Information	Belleville Chamber of Commerce (618) 233-2077
County	St. Clair

DEKALB/SYCAMORE TRAIL

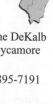

Trail Length	6 miles
Surface	Paved
Uses	Leisure bicycling, cross-country skiing, hiking
Location & Setting	The DeKalb/Sycamore Trail is 6-miles long, paved, and links the DeKalb Park District Trail from Lions Park on DeKalb's south side to Sycamore and the Great Western Trail.
Information	DeKalb County Forest Preserve (815) 895-7191
County	DeKalb

EL PASO TRAIL

Trail Length	2.7 miles
Surface	Crushed stone
Uses	Leisure bicycling, hiking
Location & Setting	El Paso
Information	Town of El Paso—City Hall (309) 527-4005
	52 North Elm, El Paso, IL 61738-4005
County	Madison

HERITAGE-DONNELLEY TRAIL

Trail Length	5 miles
Surface	Paved
Uses	Leisure bicycling, in-line skating, hiking, cross-country skiing
Location & Setting	A 5-mile paved trail running between Joliet and Lockport, forming part of the I&M Canal corridor.
Information	Will County Forest Preserve (815) 727-8700
County	Will

HUMPHREY TRAIL

Trail Length   3 miles
Surface   Paved
Uses   Leisure bicycling, in-line skating, hiking, cross-country skiing
Location & Setting The John Humphrey Trail is located in Orland Park, and connects the Village Center and Metra station. It's 3-miles long and surfaced. The setting is urban, with woods and nearby wetlands.
Information   Orland Park District   (708) 403-6115
County   Cook

JOE STENGEL TRAIL

Trail Length   11 miles
Surface   Natural
Uses   Mountain bicycling, hiking, cross-country skiing, snowmobiling
Location & Setting The 11-mile Joe Stengel Trail links Dixon & Polo using natural surface trails and roadways. The Polo trailhead is located off Judson Road.
Information   Dixon Park District   (815) 284-3308
County   Ogle, Lee

LAKE OF THE WOODS TRAIL

Trail Length   4 miles
Surface   Paved
Uses   Leisure bicycling, in-line skating, hiking
Location & Setting The Lake of the Woods Trail is paved, and is located 10-miles west of Champaign-Urbana on I-74 at Mahomet, exit #172 or #174. It passes the Early American Museum and Botanical Garden.
Information   Champaign County Forest Preserve   (217) 586-3360
County   Champaign

POPLAR CREEK TRAIL

Trail Length   9.5 miles
Surface   Asphalt
Uses   Leisure bicycling, in-line skating, jogging
Location & Setting Northwest Cook County, bordered by Hoffman Estates to the east, west and south, and South Barrington to the north. Wooded, with access to toilets, water and picnic facilities.
Information   Cook County Forest Preserve   (708)366-9420
County   Cook

PIONEER PARKWAY

Trail Length   2.5 miles
Surface   Crushed stone
Uses   Leisure bicycling, cross country skiing, hiking
Location & Setting From Peoria to Alta
Information   Peoria Park District   (309) 682-1200
County   Peoria

RONALD J. FOSTER HERITAGE PARKWAY

Trail Length	3.2 miles
Surface	Asphalt
Uses	Leisure bicycling, cross country skiing, hiking
Location & Setting	Glen Carbon
Information	Glen Carbon Village Hall	(618) 288-1200
County	Madison

NEWTON LAKE FISH & WILDLIFE AREA

Trail Length	4.5 miles
Surface	Natural
Uses	Mountain bicycling, hiking
Location & Setting	4.5 mile MBiking trail located SW of Newton in southern IL. From Newton; S on 1100E to 700N, W to 300N, S to 500N, then E to the entrance.
Information	Newton Lake Fish & Wildlife Area	(618) 783-3478
County	Jasper

RUNNING DEER TRAIL

Trail Length	3 miles
Surface	Natural – groomed
Uses	Mountain bicycling, hiking
Location & Setting	The trail is located in Dirksen Park, north of Pekin and Rte 98. The setting is wooded, and at its highest point it overlooks the Illinois River Valley.
Information	Pekin Park District	(309) 347-7275
County	Tazewell

SKOKIE VALLEY TRAIL

Trail Length	8 miles
Surface	Asphalt
Uses	Leisure bicycling, in-line skating, cross country skiing, jogging
Location & Setting	The trail parallel the west side of Hwy 41 between Old Elm Road in Lake Forest south to West Park in Highland Park. It is built on ComEd right-of-way, and there is an overpass at Half Day Road (Route 22).
Information	Lake County Dept. of Transportation	(847) 362-3950
County	Lake

WAUBONSIE TRAIL

Trail Length	2.5 miles
Surface	Paved
Uses	Leisure bicycling, in-line skating, hiking, cross-country skiing
Location & Setting	Town of Oswego, S of Aurora. Surface is asphalt, setting urban parkland.
Information	Oswego Park District	(630) 554-1010
County	Kendall

Selected Illinois State Parks

North West Region

North West Region Park Name	FACILITIES				ACTIVITIES					
	Acreage	Concession	Drinking Water	Rest rooms	Bike Trails	Boat Rentals	Canoe Access	Canoe Rental	Hiking	Camping
Argyle Lake State Park	1700	●	●	♿		●	●		●	AB/CDY
Big River State Forest	3027		♿	♿			●		●	CD
Castle Rock State Park	1995		●	●			●		●	Canoe
Delabar State Park	89		●	●			●		●	B/ECD
Hennepin Canal Parkway State Park	5773		♿	♿	●		●		♿	CDY
Ilini State Park	510	●	●	♿			●		●	B/ECY
Johnson-Sauk Trail State Park	1361	●	♿	♿		●	●		●	B/E♿DY
Jubilee College State Park	3500		♿	♿					●	AB/SC♿
Lake Le-Aqua-Na State Park	715	●	●	♿		●	●		♿	AB/SCY
Lowden State Park	2234	●	♿	♿			●		●	AB/SD
Mississippi Palisades State Park	2505	●	●	♿			●		●	AB/SDY A♿
Rock Cut State Park	3092	●	♿	♿	●	●	●		●	B/SCY
Rock Island Trail State Park	392		♿	♿	●				●	D
Starved Rock State Park	2630	♿	♿	♿			●		●	A♿YL
White Pines Forest State Park	385	♿	●	♿					●	CY

CLASS **A** SITES   Showers, electricity & vehicular access *(fee)*

CLASS **B/E** SITES   Electricity & vehicular access *(fee)*

CLASS **B/S** SITES   Showers & vehicular access *(fee)*

CLASS **C** SITES   Vehicular access *(fee)*

CLASS **D** SITES   Tent camping/primitive sites (walk in/backpack) no vehicular access *(fee)*

CLASS **Y** SITES   Youth Groups only

♿   Accessible to visitors with disabilities

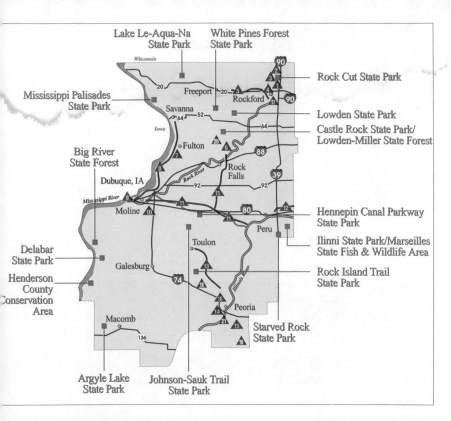

No.	Trail Name	Page #
1.	Rock Cut State Park	116
2.	Hononegah Recreation Path	73
3.	Stone Bridge Trail	121
4.	Rock River and Sportscore Recreation Path	117
5.	Pecatonica Prairie Path	106
6.	Lowell Parkway	92
7.	Fulton Bike Trail (F.A.S.T.)	57
8.	Great River Trail	62
9.	Ben Butterworth Pathway	61
10.	Kiwanis Trail	87
11.	Hennepin Canal Parkway	70
12.	I & M Canal State Trail	74
13.	Rock Island State Trail	118
14.	Pimiteoui Trail	107
15.	River Trail of Illinois	113
16.	Pioneer Parkway	134
17.	Perryville & Willow Creek Paths	26
18.	Jubilee College State Park	83
19.	Potawatomi Trail	108
20.	Joe Stengel Trail	134
21.	Running Deer Trail	135

Illinois State Parks North West Region

Selected Illinois State Parks

North East Region

North East Region Park Name	Acreage	FACILITIES			ACTIVITIES					
		Concession	Drinking Water	Rest rooms	Bike Trails	Boat Rentals	Canoe Access	Canoe Rental	Hiking	Camping
Chain O'Lakes State Park	6063	●	♿	♿	●	●	●	●		AB/SY
Channahon State Park	25		●	●	●		●		●	DY
Des Plaines Conservation Area	5012	●	●	♿			●		●	C
Gebhard Woods State Park	30		♿	●			●		●	DY
Goose Lake Prairie State Nat'l. Area	2468		●	♿					●	
I & M Canal State Trail	2802		●	●	●		●		●	D
Illinois Beach State Park	4160	♿	♿	♿	●		●		♿	A&YL
Kankakee River State Park	3932	♿	♿	♿	●		●	●	●	A&B/ECD
Moraine Hills State Park	1763	●	♿	●	●	●			●	
Silver Springs State Park	1314	●	●	♿			●	●	●	DY

CLASS **A** SITES   Showers, electricity & vehicular access *(fee)*

CLASS **B/E** SITES   Electricity & vehicular access *(fee)*

CLASS **B/S** SITES   Showers & vehicular access *(fee)*

CLASS **C** SITES   Vehicular access *(fee)*

CLASS **D** SITES   Tent camping/primitive sites (walk in/backpack) no vehicular access *(fee)*

CLASS **Y** SITES   Youth Groups only

♿   Accessible to visitors with disabilities

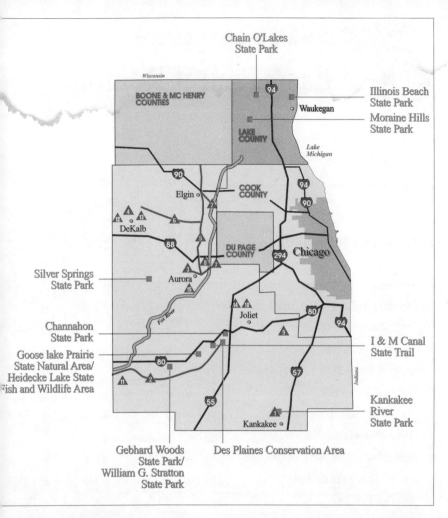

No.	Trail Name	Page #
1.	Kankakee River State Park	84
2.	I & M Canal State Trail	74
3.	Virgil L. Gilman Nature Trail	130
4.	Peace Road Trail	105
5.	Fox River Trail	54
6.	Great Western Trail	61
7.	Illinois Prairie Path	76
8.	Fermilab Bike Trail	53
9.	Old Plank Road Trail	100
10.	Centennial Trail	36
11.	Catlin Park	34
12.	Kishwaukee Kiwanis Pkwy	86
13.	DeKalb/Sycamore Trail	133
14.	Heritage-Donnelley Trail	133
15.	Waubonsie Trail	135

Illinois State Parks North East Region

East Central Region

East Central Region Park Name	Acreage	Concession	Drinking Water	Rest rooms	Bike Trails	Boat Rentals	Canoe Access	Canoe Rental	Hiking	Camping
			FACILITIES				ACTIVITIES			
Clinton Lake State Recreation Area	9915		♿	♿			●		●	B/SY
Eagle Creek State Recreation Area	1463		●	♿					●	B/ECY
Fox Ridge State Park	1517		●	♿					●	B/SY
Hidden Springs State Forest	1121		●	♿					●	CY
Kickapoo State Park	2844	●	●	♿	●	●	●	●	●	AB/SCDYR
Lincoln Trail State Park	1022	♿	●	♿		●	●	●	●	A&DY
Moraine View State Park	1688	♿	♿	♿		●	●		♿	B/ED
Walnut Point State Fish & Wildlife Area	592	●	●	♿		●	●		●	B/EDY
Weldon Springs State Park	370	●	●	♿		●	●		●	B/EDY
Wolf Creek State Park	1967		●	♿					●	RACDY

CLASS **A** SITES	Showers, electricity & vehicular access *(fee)*
CLASS **B/E** SITES	Electricity & vehicular access *(fee)*
CLASS **B/S** SITES	Showers & vehicular access *(fee)*
CLASS **C** SITES	Vehicular access *(fee)*
CLASS **D** SITES	Tent camping/primitive sites (walk in/backpack) no vehicular access *(fee)*
CLASS **Y** SITES	Youth Groups only
♿	Accessible to visitors with disabilities

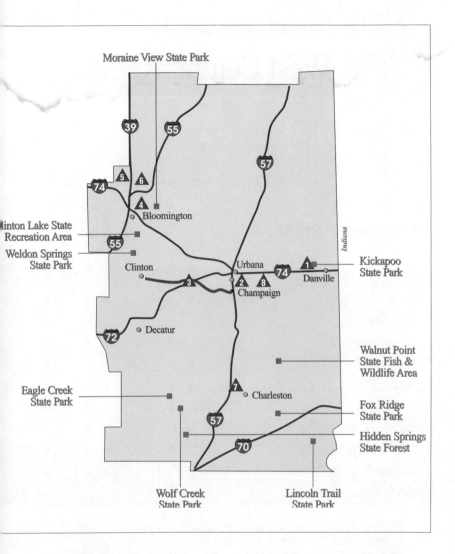

Moraine View State Park

Bloomington

Clinton Lake State
Recreation Area

Weldon Springs
State Park

Clinton

Urbana

Champaign

Kickapoo
State Park

Danville

Decatur

Walnut Point
State Fish &
Wildlife Area

Eagle Creek
State Park

Charleston

Fox Ridge
State Park

Hidden Springs
State Forest

Wolf Creek
State Park

Lincoln Trail
State Park

Indiana

No.	Trail Name	Page #
1.	Kickapoo State Park	85
2.	Champaign County	38
3.	Heartland Pathways	65
4.	Constitution Trail	44
5.	Comlara Park	43
6.	El Paso Trail	133
7.	Mattoon/Charleston Bike Path	93
8.	Lake of the Woods Trail	134

Illinois State Parks East Central Region

Selected Illinois State Parks

West Central Region

West Central Region — Park Name	Acreage	FACILITIES — Concession	Drinking Water	Rest rooms	ACTIVITIES — Bike Trails	Boat Rentals	Canoe Access	Canoe Rental	Hiking	Camping
Beaver Dam State Park	744	●	●	♿		●	●		●	AB/SY
Horseshoe Lake State Park	2854		●	♿			●		●	C♿
Nauvoo State Park	148		♿	♿			●		●	B/ECY
Pere Marquette State Park	7901	●	●	♿	●				●	A&B/SY
Randolph County State F & W Area	1021	●	●	♿		●	●		●	C♿DY
Sand Ridge State Forest	7112		●	●					●	CDY
Sangchris Lake State Park	3576	●		♿			●			B/ECDY
Siloam Springs State Park	3323	♿	♿	♿		●	●		●	A&B/SD
Washington County Conservation Area	1440	♿	♿	♿		●	●		●	A&CY
Weinberg-King State Park	772		●	♿					●	C&Y

CLASS **A** SITES — Showers, electricity & vehicular access *(fee)*
CLASS **B/E** SITES — Electricity & vehicular access *(fee)*
CLASS **B/S** SITES — Showers & vehicular access *(fee)*
CLASS **C** SITES — Vehicular access *(fee)*
CLASS **D** SITES — Tent camping/primitive sites (walk in/backpack) no vehicular access *(fee)*
CLASS **Y** SITES — Youth Groups only
♿ — Accessible to visitors with disabilities

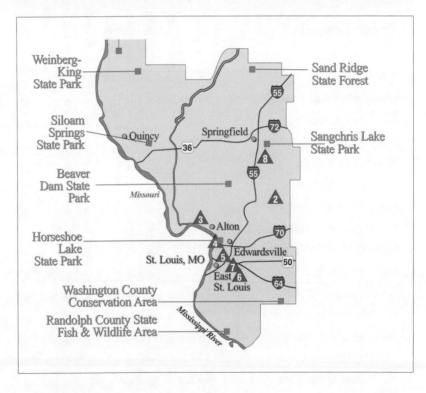

No.	Trail Name	Page #
1.	Argyle Lake State Park	30
2.	Lincoln Prairie Trail	88
3.	Vadalabene Bike Trail	126
4.	Vadalabene Nature Trail	127
5.	Delyte Morris Bicycle Way	47
6.	Belleville's Trails & Bikeways	133
7.	Ronald J. Foster Heritage Trail	135
8.	Lost Bridge Trail	89

Illinois State Parks West Central Region

Selected Illinois State Parks

South Region

South Region Park Name	Acreage	FACILITIES			ACTIVITIES					
		Concession	Drinking Water	Rest rooms	Bike Trails	Boat Rentals	Canoe Access	Canoe Rental	Hiking	Camping
Cave-in-Rock State Park	204	•	•	♿			•		•	B/ECD"
Dixon Springs State Park	787	♿	♿	♿				•	•	B/ED♿
Ferne Clyffe State Park	1125		♿	♿					•	ADY
Fort Massac State Park	1499		♿	♿			•		•	A♿B/S
Giant City State Park	3694	♿	♿	♿			•	•	♿	A♿DYL
Hamilton County Conservation Area	1683	•	•	•		•	•		•	B/EDY
Horseshoe Lake Conservation Area	9550		♿	♿			•			A♿B/E
Lake Murphysboro State Park	1024	♿	•	♿		•	•		•	A/ECY
Pyramid State Park	2528		•	•			•		•	CD
Ramsey Lake State Park	1881	•	•	♿		•	•		•	AB,ECD
Red Hills State Park	948	•	•	♿		•	•		•	A♿DY
Sam Dale Lake Conservation Area	1301	•	♿	♿		•	•		•	B/ED♿
Sam Parr State Park	1133		•	•					•	CDY
Trail of Tears State Forest	4993		•	•					•	DCY
Wayne Fitzgerrell State Park	3300	•	•	•		•		•	•	AD

CLASS **A** SITES — Showers, electricity & vehicular access *(fee)*
CLASS **B/E** SITES — Electricity & vehicular access *(fee)*
CLASS **B/S** SITES — Showers & vehicular access *(fee)*
CLASS **C** SITES — Vehicular access *(fee)*
CLASS **D** SITES — Tent camping/primitive sites (walk in/backpack) no vehicular access *(fee)*
CLASS **Y** SITES — Youth Groups only
♿ — Accessible to visitors with disabilities

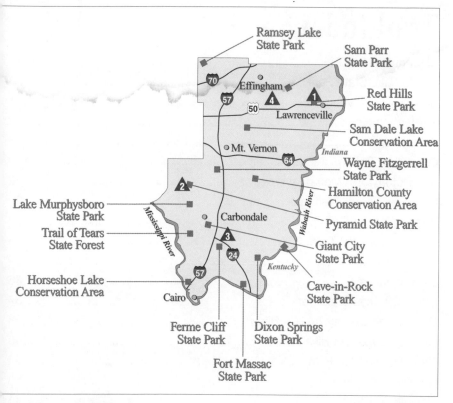

No.	Trail Name	Page #
1.	Red Hills State Park	112
2.	Pyramid State Park	111
3.	Tunnel Hill Trail	124
4.	Newton Lake & Fish Wildlife Area	134

Illinois State Parks South Region

Trail Index

Algonquin Road Trail..29
Argyle Lake State Park..30
Arie Crown Bicycle Trail..31
Bartlett's Trails 133
Batavia Spur..76
Belleville's Trails...133
Ben Butterworth Memorial Pkwy 62
Blackwell Forest Preserve 32
Buffalo Creek FP Trail..24
Busse Woods FP Trail...33
Catlin Park 34
Centennial Trail...36
Chain O'Lakes State Park 37
Champaign County Trails & Bikeways 38
Chicago Lakefront Bike Path 40
Churchill Woods FP Trail...42
Comlara Park Trail 43
Constitution Trail 44
Danada FP Trail...45
Deer Grove FP Trail 46
DeKalb-Sycamore Trail..133
Delyte Morris Bicycle Way 47
Des Plaines Division...48
Des Plaines River Trail..50
El Paso Trail..133
Evanston Paths..52
Fermilab Bike Trail 53
Fox River Trail 54
Fullersburg Woods FP 56
Fulton Bike Trail (F.A.S.T) 57
Geneva Spur..76
Grand Illinois Trail System 58
Grant Woods FP 60
Great River Trail..62
Great Western Trail 61
Great Western Trail (DuPage)...76
Green Bay Trail 64

Greenbelt Forest Preserve 65
Greene Valley FP Trail 67
Heartland Pathways 68
Hennepin Canal Parkway 70
Heritage-Donnelley Trail 133
Herrick Lake/Danada FP Trail 72
Hononegah Recreation Path 73
Humphrey Bike Trail 134
I & M Canal State Trail 74
I & M Canal Trail (Cook Cnty) 103
Illinois Beach State Park 78
Illinois Prairie Path 76
Independence Grove 79
Indian Boundary Div Trail 80
Jane Addams Trail 82
Joe Stengel Trail 134
Jubilee College State Park 83
Kankakee River State Park 84
Kickapoo State Park 85
Kishwaukee Kiwanis Pathway 86
Kiwanis Trail 87
Lake of the Woods Trail 134
Lincoln Prairie Trail 88
Long Prairie Trail 90
Lost Bridge Trail 89
Lowell Parkway 92
Mattoon to Charleston Trail 93
McDowell Grove FP Trail 94
Moraine Hills SP Trail 95
Newton Lake Fish & Wildlife Area 134
North Branch Bicycle Trail 96
North Shore Path 98
Oak Brook Bike Paths 99
Old Plank Road Trail 100
Palatine Trail & Bikeway 104
Palos & Sag Forest Preserve Trails 102
Peace Road Trail 105
Pecatonica Prairie Path 106
Perryville Path 26

Trail Index (continued)

Pimiteoui Trail 107
Pioneer Parkway...134
Poplar Creek Trail 135
Potawatomi Trail...108
Prairie Trail..109
Pratt's Wayne Wood FP 110
Pyramid State Park...111
Red Hills State Park 112
River Trail of Illinois...113
Robert McClory Bike Path 114
Rock Cut State Park 116
Rock Island State Trail...118
Rock River/Sportscore Path 117
Ronald Foster Heritage Pkwy 135
Running Deer Trail 135
Salt Creek F.P. Trail 120
Skokie Valley Trail 135
Stone Bridge Trail 121
Techny Trail Bike Path...97
Thorn Creek Bicycle Trail 122
Tinley Creek FP Trail 123
Tunnel Hill Trail..124
Vadalabene Bike Trail 126
Vadalabene Nature Trail 127
Vernon Hills Trails 128
Veteran Acres/Sterne's Woods 129
Virgil Gilman Trail...130
Walt Herrick Lippold Park 19
Waterfall Glen FP Trail 131
Waubonsie Trail 135
Willow Creek Path 27
Winding Creek Trail..19
Zion Bicycle Path 132

City to Trail Index

CITY	POP CODE	TRAIL NAME	PAGE
Albany	1	Great River Trail	62
Algonquin	4	Fox River Trail	54
Alta	1	Pioneer Parkway	134
Alton	4	Vadalabene Bike Trail	126
Annawan	1	Hennepin Canal Parkway	70
Antioch	3	Chain O'Lakes State Park	37
Arlington Hgts	5	Busse Woods FP Trail	33
Atkinson	1	Hennepin Canal Parkway	70
Aurora	5	Fox River Trail	54
Aurora	5	Virgil Gilman Trail	130
Aurora	5	Illinois Prairie Path	76
Bartlett	4	Pratt's Wayne Wood FP	110
Bartlett	4	Bartlett's Trails	133
Batavia	4	Illinois Prairie Path	76
Batavia	4	Batavia Spur	78
Batavia	4	Fox River Trail	54
Batavia	4	Fermilab Bike Trail	53
Belleville	4	Belleville's Trails	133
Bellwood	4	Illinois Prairie Path	76
Belvidere	4	Long Prairie Trail	90
Berkeley	3	Illinois Prairie Path	76
Bloomington	5	Constitution Trail	44
Bloomington	5	Comlara Park Trail	43
Bridgeport	2	Red Hills State Park	112
Brimfield	2	Jubilee College State Park	83
Brookfield	4	Salt Creek F.P. Trail	120
Buffalo Grove	4	Buffalo Creek FP Trail	24
Bureau	1	Hennepin Canal Parkway	70
Caladonia	1	Long Prairie Trail	90
Capron	1	Long Prairie Trail	90
Carpentersville	4	Fox River Trail	54
Carrier Mills	2	Tunnel Hill Trail	124
Champaign	5	Kickapoo State Park	85
Champaign	5	Heartland Pathways	68
Champaign	5	Lake of the Woods Trail	134
Champaign	5	Champaign County Trails & Bikeways	38
Channahon	3	I & M Canal State Trail	74
Charleston	4	Mattoon to Charleston Trail	93
Chicago	5	Chicago Lakefront Bike Path	40
Chicago Hgts	4	Thorn Creek Bicycle Trail	122
Clinton	3	Heartland Pathways	68
Colchester	2	Argyle Lake State Park	30
Colona	2	Hennepin Canal Parkway	70
Cordova	1	Great River Trail	62
Country Club Hills	4	Tinley Creek FP Trail	123
Countryside	3	Arie Crown Bicycle Trail	31
Crestwood	4	Tinley Creek FP Trail	123
Creve Coeur	3	River Trail of Illinois	113
Crystal Lake	4	Walt Herrick Lippold Park	19
Crystal Lake	4	Prairie Trail	109
Crystal Lake	4	Veteran Acres/Sterne's Woods	129

City to Trail Index (continued)

CITY	POP CODE	TRAIL NAME	PAGE
Crystal Lake	4	Fox River Trail	54
Crystal Lake	4	Winding Creek Trail	19
Danville	4	Kickapoo State Park	85
Darien	4	Waterfall Glen FP Trail	131
Deer Grove	2	Deer Grove FP Trail	46
Deer Park	2	Deer Grove FP Trail	46
Deerfield	4	Des Plaines Division	48
DeKalb	4	Kishwaukee Kiwanis Pathway	86
DeKalb	4	DeKalb-Sycamore Trail	133
DeKalb	4	Peace Road Trail	105
DeLand	1	Heartland Pathways	68
Des Plaines	5	Indian Boundary Div Trail	80
Des Plaines	5	Des Plaines Division	48
Dixon	4	Joe Stengel Trail	134
Dixon	4	Lowell Parkway	92
Dunlap	1	Rock Island State Trail	118
East Dundee	2	Fox River Trail	54
East Moline	4	Great River Trail	62
East Peoria	4	River Trail of Illinois	113
Edwardsville	4	Vadalabene Nature Trail	127
Edwardsville	4	Delyte Morris Bicycle Way	47
El Paso	2	El Paso Trail	133
Elgin	5	Illinois Prairie Path	70
Elgin	5	Fox River Trail	54
Elk Grove Vill	4	Busse Woods FP Trail	35
Elmhurst	4	Illinois Prairie Path	70
Elmwood Park	4	Indian Boundary Div Trail	80
Elsah	1	Vadalabene Bike Trail	126
Evanston	5	Evanston Paths	52
Flossmoor	3	Tinley Creek FP Trail	123
Forman	1	Tunnel Hill Trail	124
Fox Lake	3	Grant Woods FP	60
Fox Lake	3	Chain O'Lakes State Park	37
Frankfort	3	Old Plank Road Trail	100
Franklin Park	4	Indian Boundary Div Trail	80
Freeport	4	Pecatonica Prairie Path	100
Freeport	4	Jane Addams Trail	82
Fulton	2	Great River Trail	62
Fulton	2	Fulton Bike Trail (F.A.S.T)	57
Genesco	3	Hennepin Canal Parkway	70
Geneva	4	Fox River Trail	54
Geneva	4	Geneva Spur	70
Glen Carbon	3	Ronald Foster Heritage Pkwy	135
Glen Ellyn	4	Illinois Prairie Path	70
Glen Ellyn	4	Churchill Woods FP Trail	41
Glencoe	3	Green Bay Trail	64
Glencoe	3	North Branch Bicycle Trail	96
Glenview	4	North Branch Bicycle Trail	96
Glenview	4	Techny Trail Bike Path	96
Glenview	4	Des Plaines Division	48
Glenwood	3	Thorn Creek Bicycle Trail	122
Grafton	1	Vadalabene Bike Trail	126

Granite City	4	Vadalabene Nature Trail	127
Green Rock	2	Hennepin Canal Parkway	70
Gurnee	4	Des Plaines River Trail	50
Hampton	2	Great River Trail	62
Harrisburg	3	Tunnel Hill Trail	124
Harvard	3	Long Prairie Trail	90
Henning	1	Kickapoo State Park	85
Hickory Hills	4	Palos & Sag Forest Preserve Trails	102
Highland Park	4	Robert McClory Bike Path	114
Highland Park	4	Skokie Valley Trail	135
Highwood	3	Robert McClory Bike Path	114
Hinsdale	4	Salt Creek F.P. Trail	120
Hinsdale	4	Fullersburg Woods FP	56
Hodgkins	2	Arie Crown Bicycle Trail	31
Hoffman Estates	5	Algonquin Road Trail	29
Hoffman Estates	5	Poplar Creek Trail	135
Hudson	2	Comlara Park Trail	43
Indian Head Pk	3	Arie Crown Bicycle Trail	31
Island Lake	3	Moraine Hills SP Trail	95
Joliet	5	Heritage-Donnelley Trail	133
Joliet	5	Old Plank Road Trail	100
Kankakee	5	Kankakee River State Park	84
Karnak	1	Tunnel Hill Trail	124
Kenilworth	2	Green Bay Trail	64
LaGrange	4	Salt Creek F.P. Trail	120
LaGrange Park	4	Salt Creek F.P. Trail	120
Lake Bluff	3	Robert McClory Bike Path	114
Lake Bluff	3	North Shore Path	98
Lake Forest	4	Skokie Valley Trail	135
Lake Forest	4	Robert McClory Bike Path	114
Lansing	4	Thorn Creek Bicycle Trail	122
LaSalle	3	I & M Canal State Trail	74
Lawrenceville	2	Red Hills State Park	112
Libertyville	4	Independence Grove	79
Libertyville	4	Des Plaines River Trail	50
Libertyville	4	North Shore Path	98
Lily Lake	1	Great Western Trail	61
Lincolnshire	3	Des Plaines River Trail	50
Lincolnwood	4	North Branch Bicycle Trail	96
Lisle	4	Greene Valley FP Trail	67
Lockport	3	Centennial Trail	36
Lodge	1	Heartland Pathways	68
Lombard	4	Churchill Woods FP Trail	42
Lombard	4	Illinois Prairie Path	76
Lombard	4	Great Western Trail (DuPage)	76
Long Grove	2	Buffalo Creek FP Trail	24
Loves Park	4	Rock Cut State Park	116
Loves Park	4	Perryville Path	26
Loves Park	4	Willow Creek Path	27
Lyons	3	Centennial Trail	36
Macomb	4	Argyle Lake State Park	30
Marseilles	2	I & M Canal State Trail	74
Matteson	4	Old Plank Road Trail	100
Mattoon	4	Mattoon to Charleston Trail	93
Maywood	4	Indian Boundary Div Trail	80
Maywood	4	Illinois Prairie Path	76

City to Trail Index (continued)

CITY	POP CODE	TRAIL NAME	PAGE
McHenry	4	Prairie Trail	109
McHenry	4	Moraine Hills SP Trail	95
Melrose Park	4	Indian Boundary Div Trail	80
Milan	3	Hennepin Canal Parkway	70
Mineral	1	Hennepin Canal Parkway	70
Moline	4	Great River Trail	62
Moline	4	Ben Butterworth Memorial Pkwy	61
Moline	4	Hennepin Canal Parkway	70
Moline	4	Kiwanis Trail	87
Monticello	3	Heartland Pathways	68
Morris	4	I & M Canal State Trail	74
Morton	4	River Trail of Illinois	113
Morton Grove	4	North Branch Bicycle Trail	96
Mt. Prospect	5	Des Plaines Division	48
Mundelein	4	North Shore Path	98
Naperville	5	Greene Valley FP Trail	67
Naperville	5	McDowell Grove FP Trail	94
Naperville	5	Herrick Lake/Danada FP Trail	72
New Burnside	1	Tunnel Hill Trail	124
New Lenox	4	Old Plank Road Trail	100
Newton	2	Newton Lake Fish & Wildlife Area	134
Normal	4	Constitution Trail	44
Normal	4	Comlara Park Trail	43
Norridge	4	Indian Boundary Div Trail	80
North Aurora	3	Fox River Trail	54
North Chicago	4	Greenbelt Forest Preserve	65
North Chicago	4	Robert McClory Bike Path	114
Northbrook	4	North Branch Bicycle Trail	96
Northbrook	4	Des Plaines Division	48
Northfield	2	North Branch Bicycle Trail	96
Oak Forest	4	Tinley Creek FP Trail	123
Oakbrook	3	Fullersburg Woods FP	56
Oakbrook	3	Oak Brook Bike Paths	99
Oakbrook	3	Salt Creek F.P. Trail	120
Olney	3	Red Hills State Park	112
Olympia Fields	2	Thorn Creek Bicycle Trail	122
Orangeville	1	Jane Addams Trail	82
Orland Park	4	Humphrey Bike Trail	134
Orland Park	4	Tinley Creek FP Trail	123
Oswego	3	Waubonsie Trail	135
Ottawa	4	Catlin Park	34
Ottawa	4	I & M Canal State Trail	74
Palatine	4	Algonquin Road Trail	29
Palatine	4	Deer Grove FP Trail	46
Palatine	4	Palatine Trail & Bikeway	104
Palos Heights	4	Tinley Creek FP Trail	123
Palos Hills	4	I & M Canal Trail (Cook Cnty)	103
Palos Hills	4	Palos & Sag Forest Preserve Trails	102
Palos Park	2	Palos & Sag Forest Preserve Trails	102
Pana	3	Lincoln Prairie Trail	88
Park Forest	4	Old Plank Road Trail	100
Park Forest	4	Thorn Creek Bicycle Trail	122

Park Ridge	4	Indian Boundary Div Trail	80
Park Ridge	4	Des Plaines Division	48
Pecatonica	2	Pecatonica Prairie Path	106
Pekin	5	Potawatomi Trail	108
Pekin	4	Running Deer Trail	135
Peoria	4	Jubilee College State Park	83
Peoria	5	Pimiteoui Trail	107
Peoria	5	Rock Island State Trail	118
Peoria	5	Pioneer Parkway	134
Pinckneyville	2	Pyramid State Park	1
Polo	2	Joe Stengel Trail	134
Poplar Grove	1	Long Prairie Trail	90
Port Byron	2	Great River Trail	62
Princeton	3	Hennepin Canal Parkway	70
Princeville	2	Rock Island State Trail	118
Rapids City	1	Great River Trail	62
Richmond	2	Prairie Trail	109
Ringwood	2	Prairie Trail	109
River Grove	3	Indian Boundary Div Trail	80
Rochester	2	Lost Bridge Trail	89
Rock Falls	3	Hennepin Canal Parkway	70
Rock Island	4	Great River Trail	62
Rockford	5	Pecatonica Prairie Path	106
Rockford	5	Rock Cut State Park	116
Rockford	5	Hononegah Recreation Path	73
Rockford	5	Rock River/Sportscore Path	117
Rockton	2	Hononegah Recreation Path	73
Roscoe	2	Stone Bridge Trail	121
Roscoe	2	Hononegah Recreation Path	73
Rosemont	2	Indian Boundary Div Trail	80
Round Lk Hgts	2	Grant Woods FP	60
Savanna	2	Great River Trail	62
Schaumburg	5	Busse Woods FP Trail	33
Schiller Park	4	Indian Boundary Div Trail	80
Seneca	2	I & M Canal State Trail	74
Seymour	1	Heartland Pathways	68
Sheffield	1	Hennepin Canal Parkway	70
South Barrington	2	Poplar Creek Trail	135
South Chic Hgts	2	Thorn Creek Bicycle Trail	122
South Elgin	4	Fox River Trail	54
South Holland	4	Thorn Creek Bicycle Trail	122
Springfield	5	Lost Bridge Trail	89
St. Charles	4	Great Western Trail	61
St. Charles	4	Fox River Trail	54
St. Charles	4	Illinois Prairie Path	76
Stonefort	1	Tunnel Hill Trail	124
Sugar Grove	2	Virgil Gilman Trail	130
Sumner	2	Red Hills State Park	112
Sycamore	3	Peace Road Trail	105
Sycamore	3	Great Western Trail	61
Sycamore	3	DeKalb-Sycamore Trail	133
Tampico	1	Hennepin Canal Parkway	70
Taylorville	4	Lincoln Prairie Trail	88
Thomson	1	Great River Trail	62
Thorton	2	Thorn Creek Bicycle Trail	122
Tinley Park	4	Tinley Creek FP Trail	123

City to Trail Index (continued)

CITY	POP CODE	TRAIL NAME	PAGE
Tiskiwa	1	Hennepin Canal Parkway	70
Toulon	2	Rock Island State Trail	118
Tunnel Hill	1	Tunnel Hill Trail	124
Urbana	4	Lake of the Woods Trail	134
Urbana	4	Champaign County Trails & Bikeways	38
Utrica	1	I & M Canal State Trail	74
Vernon Hills	4	Des Plaines River Trail	50
Vernon Hills	4	Vernon Hills Trails	128
Vienna	2	Tunnel Hill Trail	124
Villa Park	4	Illinois Prairie Path	76
Villa Park	4	Great Western Trail (DuPage)	76
Virgil	1	Great Western Trail	61
Warrenville	4	Herrick Lake/Danada FP Trail	72
Warrenville	4	Illinois Prairie Path	76
Warrenville	4	Blackwell Forest Preserve	32
Warrenville	4	McDowell Grove FP Trail	94
Wasco	1	Great Western Trail	61
Waukegan	5	Greenbelt Forest Preserve	65
Waukegan	5	Robert McClory Bike Path	114
Wayne	2	Pratt's Wayne Wood FP	110
Weldon	1	Heartland Pathways	68
West Chicago	4	Illinois Prairie Path	76
West Dundee	2	Fox River Trail	54
Westchester	4	Salt Creek F.P. Trail	120
Western Springs	4	Salt Creek F.P. Trail	120
Wheaton	5	Herrick Lake/Danada FP Trail	72
Wheaton	5	Danada FP Trail	45
Wheaton	5	Illinois Prairie Path	76
Wheeling	4	Des Plaines Division	48
White Heath	1	Heartland Pathways	68
Willow Springs	2	I & M Canal Trail (Cook Cnty)	103
Willow Springs	2	Palos & Sag Forest Preserve Trails	102
Wilmette	4	Green Bay Trail	64
Winfield	3	Illinois Prairie Path	76
Winfield	3	Batavia Spur	78
Winfield	3	Herrick Lake/Danada FP Trail	72
Winfield	3	Blackwell Forest Preserve	32
Winnebago	2	Pecatonica Prairie Path	106
Winnetka	4	North Branch Bicycle Trail	96
Winnetka	4	Green Bay Trail	64
Winthrop Harbor	3	Robert McClory Bike Path	114
Winthrop Harbor	3	Illinois Beach State Park	78
Woodridge	4	Waterfall Glen FP Trail	131
Woodridge	4	Greene Valley FP Trail	67
Wyanet	2	Hennepin Canal Parkway	70
Wyoming	2	Rock Island State Trail	118
Zion	4	Zion Bicycle Path	132
Zion	4	Illinois Beach State Park	78
Zion	4	Robert McClory Bike Path	114

POP CODE: 1=under 1,000 • **2**=1,000-4,999 • **3**=5,000-9,999 • **4**=10,000-49,999 • **5**=50,000 and over

County to Trail Index

COUNTY	TRAIL NAME	PAGE
Boone	Long Prairie Trail	90
Bureau	Hennepin Canal Parkway	70
Carroll	Great River Trail	62
Champaign	Lake of the Woods Trail	134
Champaign	Heartland Pathways	68
Champaign	Champaign County Trails & Bikeways	38
Christian	Lincoln Prairie Trail	88
Coles	Mattoon to Charleston Trail	93
Cook	Palos & Sag Forest Preserve Trails	102
Cook	Bartlett's Trails	133
Cook	Algonquin Road Trail	29
Cook	Techny Trail Bike Path	97
Cook	Illinois Prairie Path	76
Cook	Green Bay Trail	64
Cook	Centennial Trail	36
Cook	I & M Canal Trail (Cook Cnty)	103
Cook	Old Plank Road Trail	100
Cook	North Branch Bicycle Trail	96
Cook	Des Plaines Division	48
Cook	Busse Woods FP Trail	33
Cook	Evanston Paths	52
Cook	Indian Boundary Div Trail	80
Cook	Deer Grove FP Trail	46
Cook	Chicago Lakefront Bike Path	40
Cook	Humphrey Bike Trail	134
Cook	Salt Creek F.P. Trail	120
Cook	Arie Crown Bicycle Trail	31
Cook	Tinley Creek FP Trail	123
Cook	Poplar Creek Trail	135
Cook	Palatine Trail & Bikeway	104
Cook	Thorn Creek Bicycle Trail	122
DeKalb	Great Western Trail	61
DeKalb	Kishwaukee Kiwanis Pathway	86
DeKalb	DeKalb-Sycamore Trail	133
DeKalb	Peace Road Trail	105
DeWitt	Heartland Pathways	68
DuPage	Oak Brook Bike Paths	99
DuPage	Fermilab Bike Trail	53
DuPage	Danada FP Trail	45
DuPage	Greene Valley FP Trail	67
DuPage	Pratt's Wayne Wood FP	110
DuPage	Waterfall Glen FP Trail	131
DuPage	Batavia Spur	78

County to Trail Index (continued)

COUNTY	TRAIL NAME	PAGE
DuPage	McDowell Grove FP Trail	94
DuPage	Great Western Trail (DuPage)	76
DuPage	Herrick Lake/Danada FP Trail	72
DuPage	Geneva Spur	76
DuPage	Centennial Trail	36
DuPage	Blackwell Forest Preserve	32
DuPage	Illinois Prairie Path	76
DuPage	Churchill Woods FP Trail	42
DuPage	Fullersburg Woods FP	56
Grundy	I & M Canal State Trail	74
Henry	Hennepin Canal Parkway	70
Jasper	Newton Lake Fish & Wildlife Area	134
Jersey	Vadalabene Bike Trail	126
Johnson	Tunnel Hill Trail	124
Kane	Fox River Trail	54
Kane	Illinois Prairie Path	76
Kane	Virgil Gilman Trail	130
Kane	Great Western Trail	61
Kendall	Waubonsie Trail	135
Lake	Greenbelt Forest Preserve	65
Lake	Illinois Beach State Park	78
Lake	Independence Grove	79
Lake	Robert McClory Bike Path	114
Lake	Grant Woods FP	60
Lake	Vernon Hills Trails	128
Lake	Buffalo Creek FP Trail	24
Lake	Skokie Valley Trail	135
Lake	Chain O'Lakes State Park	37
Lake	Zion Bicycle Path	132
Lake	Des Plaines River Trail	50
Lake	North Shore Path	98
LaSalle	I & M Canal State Trail	74
LaSalle	Catlin Park	34
Lawrence	Red Hills State Park	112
Lee	Joe Stengel Trail	134
Lee	Hennepin Canal Parkway	70
Lee	Lowell Parkway	92
Madison	Delyte Morris Bicycle Way	47
Madison	Vadalabene Nature Trail	127
Madison	Vadalabene Bike Trail	126
Madison	Ronald Foster Heritage Pkwy	135
McDonough	Argyle Lake State Park	30
McHenry	Prairie Trail	109

McHenry .... Moraine Hills SP Trail 95
McHenry .... Walt Herrick Lippold Park 19
McHenry .... Veteran Acres/Sterne's Woods 129
McHenry .... Winding Creek Trail 19
McHenry .... Fox River Trail 54
McLean .... Comlara Park Trail 43
McLean .... Constitution Trail 44
Ogle .... Joe Stengel Trail 134
Peoria .... Jubilee College State Park 83
Peoria .... Pimiteoui Trail 107
Peoria .... Rock Island State Trail 118
Peoria .... Pioneer Parkway 134
Perry .... Pyramid State Park 111
Pratt .... Heartland Pathways 68
Rock Island .... Ben Butterworth Memorial Pkwy 61
Rock Island .... Kiwanis Trail 87
Rock Island .... Great River Trail 62
Rock Island .... Hennepin Canal Parkway 70
Saline .... Tunnel Hill Trail 124
Sangamon .... Lost Bridge Trail 89
St. Clair .... Belleville's Trails 133
Stark .... Rock Island State Trail 118
Stephenson .... Jane Addams Trail 82
Stephenson .... Pecatonica Prairie Path 106
Tazewell .... Potawatomi Trail 108
Tazewell .... River Trail of Illinois 113
Tazewell .... Running Deer Trail 135
Vermilion .... Kickapoo State Park 85
Whiteside .... Hennepin Canal Parkway 70
Whiteside .... Great River Trail 62
Whiteside .... Fulton Bike Trail (F.A.S.T) 57
Will .... Heritage-Donnelley Trail 133
Will .... Kankakee River State Park 84
Will .... I & M Canal State Trail 74
Will .... Centennial Trail 36
Will .... Old Plank Road Trail 100
Williamson .... Tunnel Hill Trail 124
Winnebago .... Rock Cut State Park 116
Winnebago .... Willow Creek Path 27
Winnebago .... Perryville Path 26
Winnebago .... Rock River/Sportscore Path 117
Winnebago .... Pecatonica Prairie Path 106
Winnebago .... Hononegah Recreation Path 73
Winnebago .... Stone Bridge Trail 121
Woodford .... El Paso Trail 133

Find me a place, safe and serene,

away from the terror I see on the screen.

A place where my soul can find some peace,

away from the stress and the pressures released.

A corridor of green not far from my home

for fresh air and exercise, quiet will roam.

Summer has smells that tickle my nose

and fall has the leaves that crunch under my toes.

Beware, comes a person we pass in a while

with a wave and hello and a wide friendly smile.

Recreation trails are the place to be,

to find that safe haven of peace and serenity.

By Beverly Moore, Illinois Trails Conservancy

Illinois Bicycle Related Laws

625 ILCS 5/11-1502 TRAFFIC LAWS APPLY TO PERSONS RIDING BICYCLES Every person riding a bicycle upon a highway shall be granted all of the rights and shall be subject to all of the duties applicable to the driver of a vehicle.

625 ILCS 5/11-1503 RIDING ON BICYCLES

(a) A person propelling a bicycle shall not ride other than upon or astride a permanent and regular seat attached thereto.

(b) No bicycle shall be used to carry more persons at one time than the number for which it is designed and equipped, except that an adult rider may carry a child securely attached to his person in a back pack or sling.

625 ILCS 5/11-1504 CLINGING TO VEHICLES No person riding upon any bicycle, coaster, roller skates, sled or toy vehicle shall attach the same or himself to any vehicle upon a roadway.

625 ILCS 5/11-1505 RIDING BICYCLES UPON ROADWAY Persons riding bicycles upon a roadway shall not ride more than 2 abreast, except on paths or parts of the roadway set aside for their exclusive use. Persons riding 2 abreast shall not impede the normal and reasonable movement of traffic and, on a laned roadway, shall ride within a single lane subject to the provisions of Section 11-1505 (625 ILCS 5/11-1505).

625 ILCS 5/11-1506 CARRYING ARTICLES No person operating a bicycle shall carry any package, bundle or article which prevents the use of both hands in the control and operation of the bicycle. A person operating a bicycle shall keep at least one hand on the handlebars at all times.

625 ILCS 5/11-1507 LAMPS AND OTHER EQUIPMENT ON BICYCLES

(a) Every bicycle, when in use at night time, shall be equipped with a lamp on the front, which shall emit white light visible from a distance of at least 500 feet to the front and with a red reflector on the rear, of a type approved by the Department, which shall be visible from all distances from 100 feet to 600 feet to the rear when directly in front of lawful lower beams of headlamps on a motor vehicle. A lamp emitting a red light visible from a distance of 500 feet to the rear may be used in addition to the red reflector.

(b) A bicycle shall not be equipped with nor shall any person use upon a bicycle any siren.

(c) Every bicycle shall be equipped with a brake which will adequately control movement of an stop and hold such bicycle.

625 ILCS 5/11-1509 A uniformed police officer may at any time upon reasonable cause to believe that a bicycle is unsafe or not equipped as required by law, or that its equipment is not in proper adjustment or repair, require the person riding the bicycle to stop and submit the bicycle to an inspection and such text with reference thereto as may be appropriate.

American Bike Trails

American Bike Trails publishes and distributes
maps, books and guides for the bicyclist.

For more information:

American Bike Trails
610 Hillside Avenue
Antioch, IL 60002